SCREAMING EAGLES

101st AIRBORNE DIVISION

RUSS AND SUSAN BRYANT

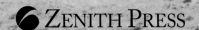

First published in 2007 by Zenith Press, an imprint of MBI Publishing Company LLC , Galtier Plaza, Suite 200, 380 Jackson Street, St. Paul, MN 55101 USA

Zenith Press titles are also available at discounts in bulk quantity for industrial or sales-promotional use. For details write to Special Sales Manager at MBI Publishing Company, Galtier Plaza, Suite 200, 380 Jackson Street, St. Paul, MN 55101 USA.

To find out more about our books, join us online at www.zenithpress.com.

Library of Congress Cataloging-in-Publication Data

Bryant, Russ, 1966–
  Screaming eagles : 101st Airborne Division / by Russ and Susan Bryant.
    p. cm.
  ISBN-13: 978-0-7603-3122-4 (softbound)
  1. United States. Army. Airborne Division, 101st—History. I. Bryant, Susan. II. Title.
UA27.5101st .B79 2007
356'.166—dc22
          2006101675

Editor: Steve Gansen
Designer: Kou Lor

Printed in China

On the cover: Sergeant First Class Arthur "Pete" Chambers of Tigerforce Scout Platoon, 1-327th Infantry Regiment, 101st Airborne Division (Air Assault), pulls security at a tactical control point during Operation Gaugamela in the city of Hawijah, Iraq, on July 20–21, 2006. *Photographer: Specialist Linsay Burnett, 1st Brigade Combat Team, 101st Airborne Division [AA] Public Affairs*

On the frontispiece: Specialist Emilio Rodriguez from the 1st Squadron, 33rd Cavalry Regiment, 3rd Brigade Combat Team, 101st Airborne Division, stands guard atop Mount Sin Jar overlooking the Syrian border. *U.S. Army photo by Staff Sergeant Russell Lee Klika*

On the title page: Soldiers from the A Battery, 3rd Battalion, 320th Field Artillery Regiment, 101st Division, stay low to the ground as a CH-47 Chinook comes in to pick them up after a morning raid in support of Operation Red Light in Remagen, Iraq, on February 24, 2006. *U.S. Navy Photo by Photographer's Mate Third Class [AW] Shawn Hussong, Fleet Combat Camera, Atlantic*

On the back cover, top right: Sergeant Michael Goodson from A Battery, 4th Battalion, 320th Field Artillery Regiment, 101st Division, performs a foot patrol in search of possible weapons caches during Operation Ten Bears in the Zafaraniyah neighborhood of Baghdad on January 23, 2006. *U.S. Army photo by Specialist Teddy Wade* **Bottom right:** Soldiers from the 3rd Battalion, 187th Infantry Regiment, along with soldiers from the Iraqi Army's 2nd Battalion, 1st Brigade, 4th Division, launch Operation Swarmer, in the Salah Ad Din province of Iraq on March 16, 2006. *U.S. Navy Photo by Journalist First Class Jeremy Wood*

About the authors:

Russ Bryant is a veteran of the 1st Ranger Battalion and F/51 Long-Range Surveillance. Following his service, Bryant attended Savannah College of Art and Design and received a bachelor's of fine art degree in photography. As a photographer, Bryant has traveled a great deal covering other non-Ranger forces of the American military. His images have appeared the *Army Times*, *Army Magazine*, *New York Times*, *Time Magazine*, and at ArmyRanger.com. Bryant is the author/photographer of a number of other Zenith Press titles, including *75th Rangers* and *USMC*.

Susan Bryant became associated with the special operations forces community when she married then–U.S. Army Ranger Russ Bryant. Since that time, she and Russ have lived in Germany and Savannah, Georgia. She was a significant researcher and contributor for photographer Russ Bryant's *To Be a U.S. Army Ranger* (MBI Publishing, 2003) and co-authored *75th Rangers* and *Weapons of the U.S. Army Rangers* (both MBI Publishing/Zenith Press, 2005). Susan holds a bachelor's degree from Furman University and master of education and education specialist degrees from Georgia Southern University. Initially a special education teacher, she now spends her days as a public school psychologist.

Contents

Chapter 1

THE MAKING OF A SCREAMING EAGLE

In 1861, among the tall white pines of Wisconsin's Flambeau River valley, a Chippewa Indian named Chief Sky plucked a four-month-old bald eagle from his nest. Chief Sky sold the young fowl to a white man for a bushel of corn. This man, in turn, resold his acquisition to Mr. Mills for a pricey five dollars. Mr. Mills had no intention of keeping the bird but gave him to Company C of the 8th Wisconsin Color Guard, a regiment of the old "Iron Brigade." In honor of Abraham Lincoln, the soldiers named the stunning eagle Old Abe. Perched upon a staff next to the unit's flying colors, Old Abe accompanied the 8th Wisconsin's men in thirty-six Civil War battles. Quickly, the unit was nicknamed the "Eagle Regiment." Twice wounded and still valiant, Old Abe was an inspiration to the soldiers. When the unit was deactivated in 1864, Wisconsin governor James T. Lewis then accepted the stoic bald eagle on behalf of the state of Wisconsin. Old Abe was featured at the Chicago Sanitary Fair that winter and later made appearances at veterans' reunions and various conventions. After twenty years of honorable service, Old Abe passed away in March 1881. Old Abe is possibly the most famous American bald eagle to ever take flight.

Following World War I, the original 101st Airborne Division shared the same Wisconsin territory as the 8th Wisconsin Regiment and the Iron Brigade—a fact that influenced the symbolism attached to the present-day 101st Airborne Division's unit insignia. The black shield background symbolizes the black iron associated with the old Iron Brigade. The eagle's profiled head refers to Old Abe. Today, the 101st Airborne Division's mascot is still the American bald eagle, but instead of being called the Eagle Regiment, they are known as the "Screaming Eagles."

The 101st Airborne Division is allocated more than 280 helicopters, which can insert a task force of four thousand soldiers hundreds of miles inside enemy territory. The division's force includes three battalions of Apache attack

A brass, sword-wielding, horse-riding statue of Saddam Hussein is engulfed in a ball of flame as it is blown from its perch outside Hussein's palatial grounds in Tikrit, Iraq, on July 18, 2003. *U.S. Army photo by Staff Sergeant Craig Pickett*

helicopters. It is equipped with far more helicopters than any other U.S. Army division, and at times even more air assets are attached to the Screaming Eagles during deployment. Such a task force comprises superior intelligence support, maintenance and operations elements, support personnel, and artillery specialists.

At the unit's activation and through the Korean Conflict era, 101st Airborne soldiers were airborne qualified, meaning that each completed the notorious Jump School located at Fort Benning, Georgia. Now renamed the Basic Airborne

Opposite: Specialist Joshua Milstead and fellow soldiers from the "War Hawks" 506th Regimental Combat Team, 101st Airborne Division, practice close-quarters battle and room clearing after confirming battle zero on their weapons. They also practice enemy-contact drills individually and as a squad while on the small-arms range at Forward Operation Base (FOB) Rustimiyah in East Baghdad, on May 10, 2006. *U.S. Navy photo by PH1 [AW] Bart A. Bauer*

Soldiers with the 502nd Infantry Regiment, 101st Airborne Division, search for a suspected terrorist camp in southwest Iraq, on September 17, 2003. *DOD photo by Private Daniel Meacham, U.S. Army*

Course (BAC), the three-week school trains and qualifies soldiers to parachute from planes flying at a low altitude.

Today's 101st Airborne infantrymen are heliborne instead of airborne. The 101st soldiers at Air Assault School learn how to insert personnel, materials, and equipment by helicopter, not by plane.

These men have answered the call to duty, on foreign soil, in the air, or on foot over treacherous terrain. Initially, airborne-qualified soldiers of the 101st Airborne Division received specific and grueling training on parachuting from large aircraft into combat territory. Now the 101st Airborne is designated as air assault and receives training to infiltrate enemy territory by means of helicopter drop. This means of insertion requires rappelling from hovering helicopters and quick maneuvers once on the ground.

Basic Combat Training

The soldier's journey to the 101st Airborne Division begins in basic combat training (BCT). Many refer to this training as simply "basic" or "basic training." All who enlist in the army complete this required eight-week course. It is the basis for all other training that the soldier will receive and transforms the civilian into a soldier.

The first week of BCT is Reception Week, when recruits arrive and get settled in their new living quarters. It takes approximately three duty days to "in-process" the new recruit. They receive haircuts, physical-training (PT) uniforms, initial uniform clothing, linens, and a handbook. Uniform nametags and alterations are ordered. The recruits are also issued identification cards and identification tags, called dog tags, which are worn every waking moment. The identification card is necessary for entrance on to secured military bases, dining facilities, and stores and services within the military post.

The recruits receive several briefings, and toward the week's end, they undergo the first of many physical training tests. They must run an eight-and-a-half-minute mile and do myriad push-ups, pull-ups, and sit-ups. They receive

Specialist Winkle (left) and Sergeant First Class Chambers (right) from the Tiger Force Scout Platoon, 1-327th Infantry Regiment, 1st Brigade Combat Team, 101st Airborne Division (Air Assault), cover both ends of the street during a cordon and search in a village in the Hawijah district, on July 17–18, 2006. *Photographer: Specialist Linsay Burnett 1st Brigade Combat Team, 101st Airborne Division [AA] Public Affairs*

instruction in barracks upkeep, because such maintenance details promote discipline, responsibility, and teamwork. Learning marching drills; how to address others; and how to salute, care for, and wear their uniform prepares them for the drill sergeant.

The drill sergeant is responsible for motivating the trainees toward success, as the army will be depending upon each of them. Drill sergeants may appear tough as nails and unable to smile at first glance. This demeanor allows for a little praise to go a long way; encouragement can be simply stated as, "Always forward, soldier." The drill sergeant, usually a staff sergeant or sergeant first class, easily commands the attention and respect of all those around him. He may appear absent of humor and great in values—the U.S. Army's seven core values.

Weeks one and two of BCT consist of classroom instruction on drill and ceremony—everything from saluting to walking and marching in parades. In the second week, training moves from the classroom to the field. Teamwork is developed as soldiers work with an assigned buddy. Individuals do not succeed at a task on their own—their buddies must succeed as well. Basic first-aid classes teach them how to care for a wounded fellow solider until medical personnel arrive. They learn map reading, land navigation, and compass use. To practice what they learn in a land-navigation course, the buddy teams must move from one point to the next according to the given azimuths, directions, and distances. (Those who do not complete the course correctly just may be late for the chow hall.) Hand-to-hand, or unarmed, combat is demonstrated then practiced.

Private First Class Daniel Frisby, 1st Squadron, 33rd Cavalry Regiment, 3rd Brigade Combat Team, 101st Airborne Division, provides security as his platoon leader gathers intelligence along the Syria/Iraq border near FOB Nimur.

This third week of training presents mounting physical and mental challenges. The physical-training demands increase to a five-kilometer foot march. Frequently, buddies will encourage and challenge one another in order to complete this run within forty-five minutes.

At Fort Benning, Georgia, thirty-foot-tall Victory Tower stands in the middle of a sandy spread—a looming threat to those who fear heights. Recruits must climb up the tower via wooden ladders and rope ladders, crossing rope bridges and scaling vertical walls on the way. At the top, an instructor helps them hook into a webbed Swiss seat with carabiners and ropes. They then rappel down a thirty-foot wall to the ground. Completion is key and not the technique or speed.

The sight of "the chamber" inspires a feeling of uneasiness in some and downright fear in others. It is the site of the nuclear biological chemical (NBC) training that mentally taxes these recruits. They are given M40 gas masks and sent, one by one, into the chamber containing CS poisonous gas. Inside, they must remove the mask and clearly pronounce their name, rank, and Social Security number to the monitoring drill sergeant (who, by the way, is fully protected with a mask). Talking without protection causes the foul gases to

Two soldiers from an Iraqi scout platoon working with the Tiger Force Scout Platoon, 1-327th Infantry Regiment, 101st Airborne Division (Air Assault), pull security at a tactical control point during Operation Gaugamela in the city of Hawijah, Iraq, on July 20–21, 2006. *Photographer: Specialist Linsay Burnett, 1st Brigade Combat Team, 101st Airborne Division [AA] Public Affairs*

fill the lungs. The soldiers must then replace their mask and clear it by blowing, similar to clearing a snorkel of water. They each run out the other end of the chamber with teary eyes, runny nose, and uncontrollable coughing. The gas burns, and the experience is forever burned in their memory.

The M40 gas mask provides respiratory, eye, and face protection against chemical and biological agents. The mask consists of a silicone-rubber face piece with an in-turned peripheral face seal and binocular rigid-lens system. A face-mounted canister (gas and aerosol filter) can be worn on either the left or the right cheek. A microphone, hose, and canister carrier are provided for combat-vehicle applications.

The focus of week four is marksmanship coupled with more physical training , which includes multiple road marches and a physical fitness test. Basic rifle marksmanship (BRM) encompasses everything the operator needs to know about the weapon, the standard issue Colt M16A2. One of the most combat-proven weapon systems in the world, the M16A2 rifle is a 5.56-millimeter caliber, lightweight, gas-operated weapon capable of semi-automatic and fully automatic operation. When properly zeroed and operated, it has

Sergeant James Bostick and fellow soldiers from the 506th Regimental Combat Team, 101st Airborne Division, demonstrate close-quarters battle techniques and drills during a training session for Iraqi Army soldiers in East Baghdad on June 28, 2006. *U.S. Navy photo by PH1 Bart A. Bauer*

Sergeant Mathew Hall of Bulldog Company, 1st Battalion, 3rd Brigade Combat Team, 187th Infantry Division, 101st Airborne, demonstrates a proper shooting stance to soldiers of the 2nd Company, 2nd Brigade, 4th Iraqi Army, at FOB Summerall, Iraq, on February 20, 2006. Training such as this is performed to ensure a more efficient Iraqi military force. *U.S. Army photo by Specialist Charles W. Gill*

Iraqi Army soldiers practice close-quarters battle drills in East Baghdad, Iraq, on June 28, 2006. The drills are being run by U.S. Army soldiers from 506th Regimental Combat Team, 101st Airborne Division. *U.S. Navy photo by Photographer's Mate First Class Bart A. Bauer*

a range of 1,000 meters. Zeroing the rifle means to align the fire-control system, or the rifle's sights, with the rifle barrel. The point of aim is the point where the bullet will impact its target with the greatest probability.

Proper rifle maintenance is crucial. After a segment of instruction and rehearsal, soldiers must disassemble and reassemble the rifle within three minutes. Soldiers are taught every part's name and function, and must recite these upon the drill sergeant's request. Before they even walk out on the firing range with a weapon, they receive a thorough orientation regarding the range operations and safety procedures. Marksmanship training involves live-fire exercises, and every safety guideline must be followed.

Shot-grouping exercises are conducted on a twenty-five-meter firing range. This method of practice emphasizes firing shot groups that are tightly placed in the same location. To be successful in this task, the soldiers must place three shots within a four-centimeter circle while standing twenty-five meters away. They are also trained to detect and engage both individual and multiple targets, or combat-type pop-up silhouettes, at distances of 75, 175, and 300 meters. The standard marksmanship test is forty targets that are

Specialist Brain Bennett, from Headquarters, Headquarters Company, 1-327th Infantry Regiment, 101st Airborne Division, helps train Iraqi Army soldiers in close-quarters combat, on FOB McHenry, Iraq, on January 2, 2006. *U.S. Army photo by Specialist Timothy Kingston*

Soldiers from the 506th Regimental Combat Team, 101st Airborne Division, demonstrate close-quarters battle techniques and drills during a training session for Iraqi soldiers in East Baghdad on June 28, 2006. *U.S. Navy photo by PH1 Bart A. Bauer*

Iraqi women line up to receive humanitarian assistance boxes from U.S. soldiers in Kamaliya, Iraq, on April 28, 2006. The soldiers are from Delta Company, 3rd Battalion, 67th Armored Regiment, 4th Brigade, 101st Airborne Division. *DOD photo by Petty Officer Second Class John T. Parker, U.S. Navy*

exposed either individually or simultaneously and at distances between 50 and 300 meters. The exercise is timed. To qualify as a marksman, soldiers must hit twenty-three of the forty targets. They must hit thirty of the forty targets to qualify as a sharpshooter and thirty-six of the forty to qualify as an expert marksman.

After four weeks, the soldiers are halfway through BCT. During the next weeks, teamwork is expanded as they work in a squad, a platoon, and a company unit.

An obstacle course is the setting for week five. Each buddy team must negotiate and clear up to twenty obstacles while running and jumping, climbing and vaulting, transversing and crawling. The obstacles include walls and rope ladders to climb, balance beams and bars to cross, and hurdles and poles to jump. The soldiers usually have to swing

Specialist Danell Herd and Private First Class Michael Ferryman of the 1st Squadron, 33rd Cavalry Regiment, 3rd Brigade Combat Team, talk with local children during a roadside break while looking for smuggling routes along the Syrian/Iraqi border.

On May 18, 2003, soldiers of the 101st Airborne Division used a translator to talk with a representative of about a hundred former Republican Guard soldiers, members of the Free Military Officers of Iraq. The group gathered outside the government building in Mosul to demand two months' back pay. The soldiers, chanted, "We give our souls, we give our blood for Iraq." *Photo by Specialist Robert Woodward, 101st Airborne Division*

on ropes and crawl under barbed wire as well. Everyone leaves the course completely covered with mud; the basic-training instructors will gladly see to this. And no one leaves the course alone. Buddy teams assist each other, but the soldiers must complete this timed event as a squad—and the squad is only as good as the slowest person.

The confidence course, such as the one found at Fort Jackson, South Carolina, is a series of twenty-four obstacles divided into four groups. The Darby Queen Obstacle Course at Fort Benning comprises twenty-six obstacles, many of which cannot be cleared without the assistance of several people.

A highlight of weeks six and seven is an extensive, untimed obstacle course that shows recruits how far they have come and how basic training has prepared them for the army. It gives them confidence in their mental and physical abilities as well as "cultivating their spirit of daring." Because they negotiate it with their company, it underscores the importance of teamwork and unity. Completing it strengthens the recruits' confidence in themselves, their platoon, their company, and the army.

Confidence-building concludes in week eight, with the ten- and fifteen-kilometer foot marches as well as a three-day field exercise that provides the soldiers with a good understanding of what combat can really be like. Live M60 machine-gun rounds blasting overhead combined with a conglomeration of artillery and small-arms fire attempt to re-create a battlefield scenario. Much of this field exercise is conducted during the night, as the company's mission is to infiltrate an enemy post. The experience clarifies just how far the soldiers have come and what lies ahead.

Graduation from BCT is an event that the soldier's family and friends do not miss. The graduates parade across the field in their Class A dress uniforms. Family members can immediately see that their loved one is not the same person who left two months ago. Instead, they find a more confident, mature, and balanced individual.

Following BCT graduation and time with family, new soldiers bid farewell to one another. They leave for various training facilities for advanced individual training (AIT), which is specific training assigned according to their military occupational specialty (MOS): cook, mechanic, clerk, engineer, medic, field artillery gunner, radio operator, and so on. Recruits generally chose their MOS at the time of enlistment, so there are few surprises when soldiers receive their training orders.

Today's infantry soldiers are exceptionally intelligent and very well trained. They use handheld computers to collect and relay information about their positions as well as the enemy's positions to their commanders miles away, all in near real time. Technological advances are continually created and tested and provide infantry soldiers with increasingly better training and equipment, such as powerful laptops, carried in their rucksacks, to pinpoint positions and perform equipment diagnostics. Soon even the weapons they carry will be computerized. Such advances become vitally important as ground troops conduct missions in urban environments. Such equipment saves lives.

Sabalauski Air Assault School

101st Airborne Division (Air Assault) School Mission: To develop technically proficient and confident soldiers capable of safely conducting immediate and sustained air assault operations.

The Air Assault School at Fort Campbell, Kentucky, has served as a grounds for training since the 1950s. Initially, the 11th Airborne Division used the area to conduct their basic airborne training. In the 1960s, the facilities were modified to host the jumpmaster school for the 101st Airborne Division. Come the early 1970s and the 101st Division's transition from an airborne to an air mobile unit, the location was utilized to teach rappelling.

Major General Sidney B. Berry, commanding general of the 101st Airborne Division from August 1973 until July 1974, established the Air Mobile School. At its inception, the school's course was five days in length. Graduates were awarded the Air Mobile Badge, which incorporated the traditional the Glider and Airborne badges. Over the years, the school's instruction has changed to reflect the unit's transition from air mobile to air assault. In 1994, the Air Assault School was renamed to honor Command Sgt. Maj. Walter J. Sabalauski.

Walter James Sabalauski was born in Lithuania in 1910 and as a small child immigrated with his family to the United States. While living in the Chicago area, he boxed professionally from 1929 to 1937. An unfortunate automobile accident ended his boxing career of thirty-three bouts, only two of them defeats. Sabalauski entered the U.S. Army in July 1941 and served in the Pacific theater during World War II, fighting on the beaches of the Solomon Islands, Guadalcanal, and the Philippines.

Sabalauski served during the Korean War with the 187th Regimental Combat Team (Airborne) and the 25th Infantry Regiment. He served three tours in Vietnam, the

Sabalauski Air Assault School Obstacle Course

Obstacle Tough One: A rope climb, a walk across an elevated beam, then a climb over and down a cargo net.

Obstacle Incline Wall: A flat wooden wall is approached by the underside, then by jumping up and grasping the top edge, pull yourself up and over the top, and either slide down the incline or jump down to the ground landing feet first.

Obstacle Low Belly Over: Mount the low log and jump to the higher log, grasping over top of log with both arms and keeping belly in contact with the log. Swing legs over log and lower body to the ground.

Obstacle Confidence Climb: Two telephone poles stuck in the ground about ten feet apart and joined by 4 x 4–inch posts forming a giant ladder that one climbs.

Obstacle Six Vaults: Using one or two hands, vault a series of six parallel logs standing approximately waist high.

Obstacle Swing, Stop, and Jump: Swing forward on a rope, stop and land standing up on a lower horizontal log. Release rope and jump to the ground.

Obstacle Low Belly Crawl: Crawl forward on belly under a matrix of wires without making contact with the wires.

Obstacle High Step Over: A series of thigh-high parallel logs are stepped over with alternating steps.

Obstacle Weaver: Two inclined ladders are positioned end-to-end to form an inverted V. With head first and chest facing up, weave body under one bar and over the next.

Sergeant Gustavo Gutierrez (front), Staff Sergeant James Auttonberry (middle), and Specialist Roger Spain (rear) from the Tigerforce Scout Platoon, 1-327th Infantry Regiment, 1st Brigade Combat Team, 101st Airborne Division (Air Assault), stand guard over a detained Iraqi man during Operation Gaugamel in the city of Hawijah, Iraq, July 20–21, 2006. *ID: 27487 Photographer: Specialist Linsay Burnett, 1st Brigade Combat Team, 101st Airborne Division [AA] Public Affairs*

first in 1963 as advisor to the 32nd Vietnamese Ranger Battalion. From Vietnam, he was sent for service in the Dominican Republic. He returned to Vietnam in 1966 and served with the 101st Airborne Division's C Company, 2nd Battalion, 502nd Infantry Regiment. During this tour, Sabalauski's actions of heroism earned him the Distinguished Service Cross and the Silver Star. During one particular mission, C Company was locating elements of the

24th North Vietnamese Regiment. Under heavy enemy fire, the company's commander called for air strikes to get the enemy battalion to break contact and withdraw. Sabalauski continually placed himself at risk to engage the North Vietnamese forces and facilitate the evacuation of American casualties.

After his second tour in Vietnam, Sabalauski served as cadet regimental sergeant major at the U.S. Military Academy in West Point, New York. In 1968, he returned to Vietnam for his third and final tour, serving with the 2nd Battalion, 502nd Infantry Regiment. His military career concluded upon his retirement in 1971. Over the course of his thirty-year service, Sabalauski earned the Distinguished Service Cross, Silver Star, Legion of Merit, eight Bronze Stars, three Air Medals, six Army Commendation Medals, four Purple Hearts, three Awards of the Combat Infantryman's Badge, the Master Parachutist Badge, and campaign medals for service in World War II, Korea, the Dominican Republic, and Vietnam. Sabalauski died in 1993 and was buried with full military honors in Arlington National Cemetery.

On December 17, 1999, the new Sabalauski Air Assault School was dedicated, and for the first time in several years, all phases of air -assault instruction, plus other courses of instruction, were conducted at one facility. The Sabalauski Air Assault School trains leaders and soldiers assigned to the 101st Airborne Division, as well as other army units and U.S. Armed Services units. Its courses include Air Assault, Pathfinder, Pre-Ranger, Basic Airborne and Jumpmaster Refresher, Rappel Master, and Fast Rope Insertion Extraction System/Special Purpose Insertion Extraction System (FRIES/SPIES) Master. It also serves as the home to the 101st Division's Parachute Demonstration Team.

Private First Class Andrew Gaffrod from 2nd Platoon, Alpha Company, 1st Battalion, 327 Infantry, 101st Airborne, talks with Iraqi soldiers prior to conducting a joint foot patrol in the village of Namla, Iraq, on October 31, 2005. *U.S. Air Force photo by Technical Sergeant Andy Dunaway*

Curious civilians crowd around an armed vehicle and attempt to converse with a soldier from 1st Brigade, 101st Airborne Division, in Najaf, Iraq. The citizens of Najaf were quick to express their gratitude, welcoming their liberators with open arms. *Photo by Private First Class James Matise/U.S. Army*

The Air Assault Course

The school's Air Assault course is a fast-paced, two-week course designed to teach air-assault skills and improve leadership qualities. It is guaranteed to provide each attendee with tough mental and physical challenges.

Preparations for the Air Assault course begin months in advance. Soldiers have to have a recent medical exam specifically stating they are "qualified for Air Assault." Due to the intense physical demands, soldiers must earn passing marks on the Army Physical Fitness Test prior to entering the Air Assault course. Many candidates actually train on the Sabalauski Air Assault School obstacle course as preparation for the upcoming challenges. If candidates do not have access to the actual obstacle course, the individual's

unit often conducts some type of ongoing and appropriate physical training.

Soldiers receive a packing list of items that are either required, optional, or prohibited for the duration of the course. Soldiers missing any required item from the packing list may not be allowed to attend. Likewise, use or possession of disallowed items may warrant dismissal or other consequences. For instance, students aren't allowed cell phones on the school's grounds. All soldiers must wear the issued ballistic-type Kevlar helmet or the standard patrol cap during the training; no unit berets are allowed. They can't wear civilian contact lenses and eyeglasses; only military-issued corrective eyewear is allowed. Dog tags and identification cards must be carried at

continue on page 22

Major Steve Manley (right), the 101st Airborne Division's senior physician's assistant, converses with two Iraqi women outside a local healthcare clinic. The division distributed truckloads of medical supplies to several local facilities to replace supplies consumed during the fighting or taken by looters. *Photo by Private First Class James Matise/U.S. Army*

Captain Shelia Matthews meets with the fuel committee chairman for the Karradah district of Baghdad, August 24, 2006, to discuss an improvement project for the Karradah district propane station. Matthews is the civil-military operations officer for the 4th Battalion, 320th Field Artillery Regiment, 506th Regimental Combat Team, 101st Airborne Division. *U.S. Navy photo by Mass Communication Specialist First Class Keith W. DeVinney*

Soldiers from the Iraqi Army's 1st Brigade, 6th Division, raised their rifles in celebration after graduating the basic course of first Commando Company at FOB Justice, Iraq.

Private First Class Richard Robinson, Bravo Company, 1st Battalion, 187 Infantry Regiment, 3rd Brigade Combat Team, 101st Airborne, scans a corner of a house while conducting a foot patrol in the city of Bayji, Iraq, on December 10, 2005. *U.S. Air Force photo by Technical Sergeant Andy Dunaway*

Continued from page 19
all times. Upon arrival on "Zero Day," all soldiers' bags are checked and the preparedness test begins.

To qualify for the Air Assault course, candidates must first successfully complete the school's obstacle course. The obstacle course allows the school's keen instructors to recognize students who are potentially afraid of heights or easily unnerved in stressful situations before the training intensifies in the coming days. After safety demonstrations and stretching exercises, the candidates line up at the course's start point and begin negotiating the course. They must successfully complete the first two obstacles and pass six of the remaining seven obstacles to receive a "go" on the course itself. Each individual has two chances to pass each obstacle.

Rappel Master

It is the Rappel Master who instructs the air assault soldiers in the proper and safe technique of rappelling from ground, towers, and aircraft. The candidate becomes a Rappel Master after successful completion of the five-day Rappel Master course. The Rappel Master is not only a graduate of Air Assault School but must come highly recommended by his or her commander. Each Rappel Master meets height, weight, hearing, and fitness standards.

The Rappel Master course teaches rappelling techniques and procedures, and qualifies soldiers to serve as rappel masters during ground and aircraft rappelling. The Rappel Master students learn far more than the actual rappelling techniques. During the course candidates receive instruction on the duties and responsibilities of a rappel master; inspection, rigging, and maintenance of rappel equipment; common knots utilized during rappel operations; hook-up procedures; inspection of rappel seats tied on rappellers; rigging a rappel point on ground and aircraft; and aircraft command and control during rappelling.

Students are evaluated throughout the course and are tested on every aspect taught. In order to successfully complete this course, student must score 70 percent or better on the written test. On the equipment inspection evaluation, the candidate is given five items of equipment to inspect thoroughly and must identify the unserviceable equipment items within two minutes. The knot test requires students to tie correctly the following knots, each in thirty second or less: anchor line bowline with overhand knot, square knot with two overhand knots, prusik knot with overhand knot, and bowline with overhand knot. Hook-up test mandates students to inspect two hook-ups, each within ten seconds, and identify any deficiencies.

Rappel Master Personnel Inspection (RMPI), another aspect of evaluation, is the physical inspection of the soldier preparing for a rappel prior to its execution. Given three rigged rappellers, the Rappel Master student must inspect all three rappellers within three minutes and thirty seconds and must identify all of the major and all but two of the minor deficiencies in order to pass this area. One of the three rappellers is rigged without combat equipment ("Hollywood" style). The second one is rigged to rappel with his weapon and load-bearing equipment or a load-bearing vest (semi-combat mode). The third rappeller for inspection is rigged with his weapon, rucksack or another pack, and load-bearing equipment or a load-bearing vest (combat mode).

In regard to aircraft rigging, the Rappel Master students correctly rig a UH-60 Blackhawk helicopter for rappelling operations within five minutes. To satisfy the aircraft command and control tasks, candidates actively issue commands, use proper hand and arm signals, and correctly perform all procedures controlling rappellers from a UH-60 Blackhawk helicopter in flight.

Students are permitted one retest per exam. Students who fail a retest are dropped from the course. Safety and security of personnel, equipment, and materials are vitally important and responsibility lies on the Rappel Master to properly train future soldiers. These tasks taught during the Rappel Master course are the same skills that each Air Assault soldier must master. Upon Rappel Master course graduation, soldiers are qualified to train rappellers, inspect rigged rappellers, and conduct ground and aircraft rappelling operations.

Staff Sergeant Jason Lyday, Headquarters, Headquarters Company, 1st Battalion, 327 Mortars Platoon, 101st Airborne, demonstrates how to handle the AK-47 in close-quarters battle as part of a weapons class for the Iraqi soldiers at FOB McHenry, Iraq, on November 21, 2005. *U.S. Air Force photo by Technical Sergeant Andy Dunaway*

No matter how tired they become, soldiers are expected to double-time between obstacles while sounding off with an exuberant "Air Assault" every time their left foot hits the ground. The school's instructors add to the challenge by demanding physical exercises such as flutter kicks and push-ups between the obstacles.

The obstacles, in order of their appearance on the course, are: Tough One, Incline Wall, Low Belly Over, Confidence Climb, Six Vaults, Swing Stop Jump, Low Belly Crawl, High Step Over, and Weaver. These obstacles test the soldier's upper-body strength, grip strength, physical endurance, agility, and self-confidence. Confident soldiers in excellent physical condition are less likely to become a safety risk to themselves, their fellow students, and their instructors.

A two-mile run in army boots is next on the agenda after a brief rest break. Set at the pace of a ten-minute mile, this formation run must be completed in eighteen minutes or less. Only those who pass the obstacle course and complete the run are officially enrolled in the Air Assault course. Approximately 10 to 15 percent of the hopeful candidates do not make it past Zero Day and instead must return to their units.

The Air Assault course includes some classroom instruction, but the majority of it is performance orientated, with numerous demonstrations and opportunities for practical application. The course is divided into four graded training phases: Combat Air Assault Operations, Sling Load Operations, Rappelling, and Road March. Soldiers must receive a passing score on the written and practical

A destroyed Iraqi weapons cache in Dog East, a major battle site near Al Najaf. *Photograph by Lieutenant John Gay, Coalition Press Information Center*

At a local checkpoint in east Baghdad, Captain John Madia of the "Archangels" from the 4th Battalion, 320th Field Artillery, 4th Brigade, 506th Regimental Combat Team, 101st Airborne Division, meets with an Iraqi officer to receive an update and offer assistance, on July 27, 2006. The bullet-ridden windshield of an Iraqi Army vehicle is evidence of the small-arms fire Iraqi Army members frequently receive from insurgents. *U.S. Navy photo by MC1 Keith W. DeVinney*

application examinations at the end of each phase in order to be awarded the Air Assault Badge. During the Air Assault course, attendees have daily physical training, including the standard three-mile distance run.

During the first phase, Combat Air Assault Operations, soldiers are trained and tested on various aspects that assure mission completion, equipment security, and personnel safety. This phase is three days in duration. The class is taught air-assault operations and pathfinder operations. Soldiers learn army helicopter characteristics and capabilities, aircraft safety, hand and arm signals for guiding aircraft, and medical evacuation procedures. Featured U.S. Army rotary-winged aircraft include the UH-60 Blackhawk, MH-47 Chinooks, AH-64 Apaches, and UH-1 "Huey" choppers. Instruction continues with the roles and duties of infantry, aviation, fire support, engineers, and intelligence and support units in the air-assault mission. The candidates actively demonstrate their knowledge of hand and arm signals in a testing situation. They are also given a written examination on which they must score 70 percent correct or better. Students participate in an orientation flight in a UH-60 Blackhawk helicopter that demonstrates the three terrain flight modes. Phase one also includes continuing physical training, a road march, and a combat air-assault operation itself.

Private First Class Heath Stachar, from the Military Integrated Transitional Team, 101st Airborne Division, provides rooftop security for a ceremony on FOB Dagger in Tikrit, Iraq, on August 8, 2006. The ceremony marks the 4th Iraqi Army Division taking the security lead for the provinces of Sulymaniya, Salah Ah Din, and Kirkuk. With the assumption of these responsibilities, Iraqi security forces' control of Iraq reached the 50 percent mark. *U.S. Army photo by Staff Sergeant Russell Lee Klika*

First Lieutenant Jason Hehl, an S-4 officer for the 3rd Battalion, 187th Infantry Regiment, 3rd Brigade Combat Team, 101st Airborne Division, provides security for soldiers of the 310th Tactical Psychology Company as they talk with shop owners in the city of Samarra, Iraq.

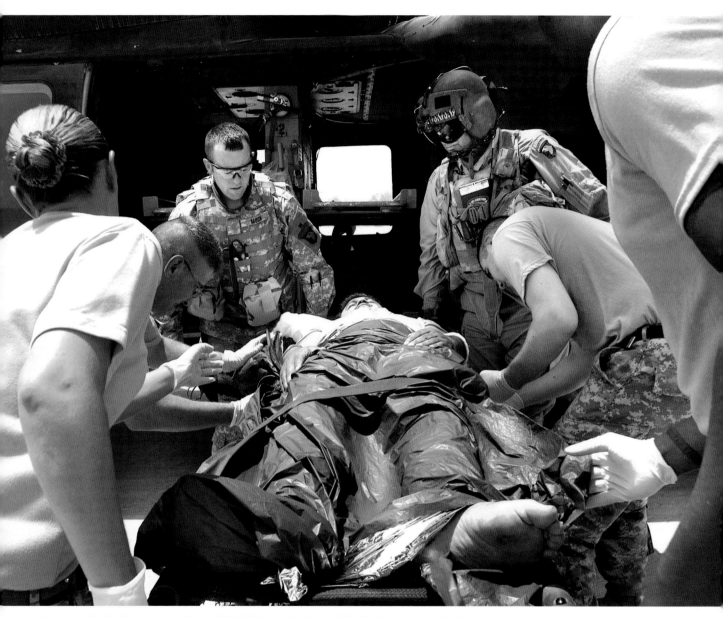

A wounded Iraqi soldier is unloaded from a UH-60A Blackhawk at the 47th Combat Support hospital in Mosul on July 20, 2006. The Blackhawk crew is from 1st Forward Support Medical Team, 542nd Medical Company (Air Ambulance). The soldier suffered a gunshot wound to the leg. *U.S. Air Force photo by Staff Sergeant Jacob N. Bailey*

Phase two, Sling Load Operations, is three and a half days and considered the most difficult phase of the Air Assault course. It begins with a road march and moves to intense training. Sling Load Operations encompasses how to prepare, rig, and inspect sling loads for transportation by army helicopters. Sling loads are equipment secured with specifically tied, tried-and-true knots that support the load's weight. A sling load can be a specific vehicle such as a M998 HMMWV "Humvee" or mounted artillery piece like a

M101A1 Howitzer. A sling load may be a five-thousand- or ten-thousand-pound cargo net of supplies, an A-22 cargo bag, or multifuel blivets, all needing transport to another battlefield location. Students must memorize information such as the tensile strength of the equipment, lift capabilities of the rotary-winged aircraft, and how to rig and inspect the sling load. Students implement the newly acquired knowledge in a practical field exercise on the Light Fighter PZ (pick-up zone), using the UH-60 Blackhawk as the lift aircraft

Sergeant Gustavo Gutierrez, a team leader for the Tigerforce Scout Platoon, 1-327th Infantry Regiment, 101st Airborne Division (Air Assault), guards a tactical control point with a soldier from an Iraqi scout platoon during Operation Gaugamela in the city of Hawijah, Iraq, July 20–21, 2006. *Photographer: Specialist Linsay Burnett, 1st Brigade Combat Team, 101st Airborne Division [AA] Public Affairs*

and the A-22 cargo bag as the load. Each soldier develops his own procedure for inspections and is tested on the ability to correctly inspect a load. A correct inspection will identify at least three of four possible deficiencies within two minutes per sling load. Students must work with speed and accuracy. To receive a passing score, the student must correctly inspect four of six sling loads. Finally, each student must again score 70 percent or better on a written examination.

During the third phase, Rappelling, soldiers begin their instruction on the ground, learning about the basic rappelling equipment, hooking into a rappel rope, appropriate hand and arm signals, belay procedures, and knot tying. This knot-typing instruction includes how to tie a hip rappel seat,

which was once called the Swiss seat. Soldiers are taught to tie a series of knots that can physically support themselves and their personal combat equipment during air infiltrations and exfiltrations. Ground training includes rappelling off an incline ramp to safely practice these skills.

Each individual learns the basic Hollywood rappel, the combat-equipment rappel, the Hollywood lock-in rappel, and the combat-equipped lock-in rappel. Training continues on the side of a tower, both with and without combat equipment. Soldiers perform a series of rappels from walls and helicopters. Beginning at the top of the tower, they rappel down one of the tower's side walls. They then rappel down an open side of the tower, simulating rappelling or fast-roping

First Sergeant William Wilder (center) gives a handful of candy to an Iraqi girl during a foot patrol break in Mahmodyah, Iraq, on April 12, 2006. Wilder and his fellow soldiers are attached to Delta Company, 1st Battalion, 502nd Infantry Regiment, 2nd Brigade, 101st Airborne Division. *DOD photo by Senior Airman Desiree N. Palacios, U.S. Air Force*

techniques from an actual helicopter. Candidates must also successfully complete three daytime and two nighttime rappels from UH-60 Blackhawk helicopters hovering 70 to 100 feet above the ground. Each candidate must also ascend and descend the troop ladder on a thirty-five-foot tower and a CH-47 helicopter.

Again, at the phase's end, the candidates are tested on what they have learned. Students must correctly tie a hip-rappel seat in ninety seconds and hook up to a rappel rope within fifteen seconds. They must execute also three rappels: Hollywood, Hollywood lock-in, and combat equipment.

To finish the course and earn the respected Air Assault Badge, candidates must successfully complete a twelve-mile road march in three hours or less. On the road march, each soldier dons full combat gear with load bearing equipment (LBE), a twenty-five- to thirty-pound rucksack, a Kevlar

helmet, and an M-16 rifle. At the end of the march, the students' bags are inspected, and if they are missing any items from the packing list, they are given a road march "no-go," or a failing score. A no-go means a duffel-bag drag: unsuccessful soldiers drag their packed duffel bags out the door and back to their home units.

Approximately 90 percent of the typical Air Assault class graduates. Sometimes, candidates are given a second opportunity to pass a task, but sometimes second chances are like wishes in the wind. The standards are high. In some instances, such as when a severe injury or illness prevents a soldier from participating in or completing a phase, a soldier may be allowed restart the phase.

In addition to Sabalauski Air Assault School in Kentucky, Air Assault courses are conducted at Schofield Barracks, Hawaii; Fort Drum, New York; and various locations across

Private First Class Janelle Zalkovsky hands out humanitarian-aid items to local citizens in Thyad, Iraq, on December 4, 2005. Zalkovsky is attached to the Civil Affairs Unit of the 1st Battalion, 320th Field Artillery Regiment, 101st Airborne Division. *DOD photo by Specialist Charles W. Gill, U.S. Army*

the United States and overseas. For instance, in September 2003, nineteen instructors from the Sabalauski Air Assault School established a training course for 101st Airborne Division's soldiers stationed in a combat zone at Qayyarah West Airfield, Iraq. They brought all of the equipment they could carry and established a secure perimeter near the airfield so the training candidates could focus upon the training. Some soldiers stationed in Iraq had not had the time to attend the Air Assault course. Younger soldiers with the 101st Division were conducting some air-assault operations in a combat zone without the benefit of the formal training. Candidates at the overseas Air Assault courses are held to the same high standards and training as those attending courses in the United States. They follow the same daily training schedule from four o'clock in the morning until eight o'clock in the evening. The training course in Iraq lasts

six days instead of the usual ten and excludes the road marches and obstacle course, except for the rope climb.

The Pathfinder Course

Pathfinder operations establish landing zones (LZs), pick-up zones (PZs), and drop zones (DZs) for troops arriving via airborne insertion. The three-week U.S. Army Pathfinder School at Fort Benning, Georgia, trains soldiers in a variety of skills needed for these operations. Over the course of the modern U.S. military's history, pathfinder units and formal training courses have come and gone. In 1955, the school was reopened under the Airborne–Air Assault branch of the Infantry School to re-establish training operations. Today's Pathfinder School is available to qualified applicants, either enlisted personnel or officers, usually those with an MOS related to infantry, aviation,

Along Iraq's Sin jar Mountain Range, a Yezidis woman listens to soldiers from the 1st Squadron, 33rd Cavalry Regiment, 3rd Brigade Combat Team, 101st Airborne Division.

scouting, or communications, who require pathfinder skills. All Pathfinder School students have to pass a valid Pathfinder physical and be cleared to participate in airborne operations. Pathfinder School candidates must not have a speech impediment.

Today's Pathfinders are trained in airborne, small boat, vehicle, foot, and sometimes freefall infiltration techniques. They may be expected to coordinate aircraft movement, control parachute drops of personnel and equipment, conduct sling-load operations, and provide initial weather information to commanders. Students hone their navigational skills—learning to navigate both with and without the use of modern technology—or dismounted navigation. Furthermore, they provide basic air-traffic control techniques and navigational assistance to airborne operations.

Soldiers quickly carry an injured serviceman toward a UH-60 Blackhawk helicopter in Baghdad on August 26, 2004. The helicopter will carry the injured soldier to a combat support hospital for medical treatment. *DOD photo by Staff Sergeant D. Myles Cullen, U.S. Air Force*

Brass shell casings lie scattered in the road as soldiers from Alpha Troop, 1st Battalion, 75th Cavalry Squadron, 101st Airborne Division, provide security after an altercation in Baghdad on February 22, 2006. *DOD photo by Specialist Timothy W. Story, U.S. Army*

Pathfinder students learn to establish, mark, and operate helicopter landing and parachute drop zones during the day and night. They learn to survey the site, provide security, and mark the drop zone for the follow-on forces. They learn to give the aviator the proper information so the parachutists are released over the drop zone at the appropriate time. The release of the airborne personnel is dependent upon wind speed, weather, the drop zone's size, and the number of personnel and aircraft. Therefore, the pathfinder student must learn how and when to use computed air release points (CARPs), the ground-marking release system, the Army Aircraft Verbal Initiated Release System, and the PIBALL (pilot balloon) meteorological instrument to measure mean effective wind. Near the course's end, students participate in a three-day field training exercise as a member of a Pathfinder team and in the graded positions of team leader and assistant team leader.

A UH-60 Blackhawk helicopter descends to extract U.S. soldiers from an area west of FOB Summerall, Iraq, during operations on June 9, 2006. The soldiers are attached to the 1st Battalion, 187th Infantry Regiment, 101st Airborne Division. *DOD photo by Specialist Charles W. Gill, U.S. Army*

Chapter 2

THE SCREAMING EAGLES IN NORMANDY

American paratrooper, among the first to make successful landings on the continent, holds a Nazi flag captured in a village assault, Utah Beach, St. Marcouf, France, June 8, 1944. *U.S. Army photo*

Over the years, the 101st Airborne Division has demonstrated superb tactical mobility and strategic response to the army's need for swift insertion behind enemy lines during tumultuous situations worldwide. As the U.S. Army's unequaled air-assault division, the 101st Airborne Division provides forcible entry into enemy territory by means of heliborne operations. Its strength and capability puts the unit in high demand during combat operations.

Opposite: Dwight Eisenhower gives orders to American paratroopers in England. *Library of Congress*

On August 19, 1942, the 101st Airborne Division was activated at Camp Claiborne, Louisiana; Major General William "Bill" Carey Lee was the unit's first commander. At the unit's activation ceremony, Lee explained to the newly inducted soldiers that the 101st Airborne was without a history, but was certain to have a "rendezvous with destiny." Only the toughest men were allowed to serve in the division. Only one in three passed the qualification criteria, which included a three-day, 140-mile foot march in addition to the intense airborne training. Only those who "died a thousand deaths" in training would be able to call themselves Screaming Eagles of the 101st.

The haystack at right would have softened the landing for this paratrooper who hit the earth head first during operations in Holland by the 1st Allied Airborne Army, September 24, 1944. *U.S. Army photo*

In October 1942, the new recruits to the 101st Airborne Division were sent to Camp Mackall at Fort Bragg, North Carolina, for the airborne infantrymen's infamously rigorous training. There they learned how to parachute from an airplane and how to successfully fight the land war behind enemy lines. The intense training prepared the soldiers in basic infantry skills, parachute techniques, and insertion by glider plane. Initially, the parachute troops and glider troops trained separately, but in early 1943 both types of troops began training together. When the 101st Airborne Division was formed, it consisted of the following core units: 502nd Parachute Infantry Regiment (PIR), 327th and 401st Glider Infantry Regiments (GIR), and three artillery battalions (377th Parachute Field Artillery, 321st Glider Field Artillery, and 907th Glider Field Artillery). Additional support units were 326th Airborne Engineer Battalion, 101st Signal Company, 326th Airborne Medical Company, and 426th Airborne Quartermaster Company.

After the 2nd Army maneuvers training exercise in Tennessee during June 1943, elements of the 101st Airborne Division, which included the 501st Parachute Infantry Regiment (PIR), were certified as ready for battle. The invasion of Nazi-occupied Europe was on the horizon, and the 101st Division was to become an instrumental force.

The 101st Airborne Division left Camp Shanks, New York, for England on September 4, 1943. There were 5,800

The members of the 101st Airborne Division, right, are on guard for enemy tanks on the road leading to Bastogne, Belgium. They are armed with bazookas, December 23, 1944. *U.S. Army photo*

101st Division men aboard their overseas vessel, the SS *Strathnaver*. Soon after departure, problems arose, and the vessel docked at St. John's, Newfoundland. Eventually, the men of the 101st Division transferred to the SS *John Ericsson* and set sail from Halifax, Nova Scotia, on October 4, 1943, arriving in Liverpool, England, on October 18, 1943. The 506th PIR sailed for the United Kingdom separately on the SS *Samaria* and had arrived weeks earlier.

Preparations for combat continued on English shores. In Berkshire and Wiltshire, about eighty miles from London, advanced training prepared the soldiers in night operations, urban warfare, German equipment identification, and land navigation.

Soon after the 101st Airborne Division arrived in England, it became evident that key personnel in non-parachute support units (such as doctors, chaplains, and forward-artillery observers) would also need to qualify as parachutists. The 101st Airborne Division established the 101st Parachute Jump School on October 12, 1943, in the 502nd PIR's encampment area in the Wiltshire village of Chilton Foliat to train and certify these auxiliary personnel. Training began November 7, 1943, and by June 1944, four hundred key support personnel were qualified as parachutists.

In January 1944, the division's battle-ready fighting force comprised three parachute infantry regiments (the 501st,

Members of the 101st Airborne Division walk past dead comrades who were killed during the Christmas Eve bombing of Bastogne, Belgium, the town in which this division was besieged for ten days. This photo was taken on Christmas Day, 1944. *U.S. Army photo*

502nd, and 506th) and two glider infantry regiments (the 327th and 401st).

Not long after, Major General Lee suffered a heart attack that forced him to relinquish command of his beloved 101st Airborne Division. Lee was and is warmly referred to as the "Father of the U.S. Airborne." It is said that the paratroopers he trained honored him by shouting out "Bill Lee" as the jumped out of their planes on D-day, during the parachute drops that Lee had helped plan. Replaced by Major General Maxwell D. Taylor, former division artillery commander of the 82nd Airborne Division, Lee returned stateside, to his

birthplace and hometown of Dunn, North Carolina, where he died on June 25, 1948. (Today, Dunn is the location of the General William C. Lee Airborne Museum.)

On March 24, 1944, a demonstration of American military fighting power was staged for top English and American brass, including English prime minister Winston Churchill and supreme Allied commander General Dwight D. Eisenhower. American forces proudly displayed their latest fighting asset: the troops of the 101st Airborne Division. The division earned astounding approval and utmost respect among the Allied commanders and troops. Subsequently,

Troops of the 101st Airborne Division watch C-47's drop supplies to them, December 26, 1944. *U.S. Army photo*

Division Commander Taylor was given orders to enter the war in Europe with the invasion of the coast of Normandy, France. The 101st Division paratroopers prepared for a large-scale night operation. Their mission: to land behind the German lines and clear the exit points from Utah Beach for the massive Allied forces beach assault and follow-on forces of the U.S. Army 4th Infantry Division.

The Invasion of Normandy

On June 5, 1944, at 10:15 p.m., soldiers of the 101st Airborne Division began their flight from several English airfields aboard nearly five hundred C-47 transport aircraft.

The planes circled England for nearly two hours while falling into their V formations. Just after midnight, the planes crossed the English Channel, and immediately, challenges began for the pilots. A dense fog had covered the area, making visibility poor. The previously dropped Pathfinder teams marked some but not all of the designated drop zones in time for the division's arrival. To complicate matters, heavy enemy antiaircraft fire caused pilots to take evasive action and break formation to avoid being hit. Paratroopers jumped at precarious altitudes and air speeds, such as an altitude of 300 feet and a speed of 200 miles per hour versus a desirable altitude of 700 feet at 100 miles per hour. The

Author's Journal, by Susan Bryant

May 26, 1990

We left the Robinson Barracks' USO in Stuttgart, West Germany, by tour bus in the late afternoon after everyone was dismissed for the long Memorial Day weekend and holiday. Russ and I thought it would be only fitting to spend the weekend touring Normandy, France, and the historic sites of D-day. At first, everyone in the bus was chattering and joking around. Several guys from Russ's unit were on the tour as well as many people we did not even know. As darkness fell, the bus grew quiet and several of us dozed. We woke to the bright sunlight streaming across the Norman countryside and bouncing off the English Channel. Before us stood the Benedictine Abbey of Mont Saint-Michel. It consumed its entire island and was easily surrounded by water in the high tide. From the distance, the stone and steeples appeared surreal against the brilliant blue sky. The village still surrounds the abbey, and obviously this historic structure was untouched by the D-day events of 1944. The tour spent the morning at Mont Saint-Michel, and I could have spent several days in the magnificent splendor of such architecture.

Aboard the bus we traveled to the French town Bayeux to visit the cathedral, view the infamous Bayeux Tapestry, and spend the night. It is a sincere blessing that the Bayuex Cathedral was spared from the relentless Allied bombing raids in 1944. I spent my afternoon walking about the cathedral and soaking in its grandeur. I never made it over to see the tapestry in a nearby building.

May 27, 1990

After a quick continental breakfast of fresh bread and butter, cheese, sliced meats, and strong coffee, Russ and I stepped out of the Bayeux inn and down a nearby walking path. The air teemed with old world sights and sounds: cow bells and bleating sheep, peaceful meadows, rolling hills dotted with leafy trees, colorful flowers. What an experience it must have been for the French when such serenity was blasted to bits by the eruption of bombing raids, artillery, and rifle fire. How disturbing it must have been when the Germans came and took their provisions, livelihood, and personal sense of security. The bus rolled past quaint farmhouses, grazing pastures, and stone walls until we arrived in the small town of Sainte-Mere-Eglise. This was our first stop in a day-long tour of the Normandy D-day invasion sites. I found it only fitting that this was our starting point since Sainte-Mere-Eglise was the first liberated French town of World War II.

Grey cobblestones covered what appeared to be a town square or church yard. Directly next to the open paved area was the church of Saint Mere-Eglise. Its exterior was not as fortunate as the Bayeux Cathedral or Mont Saint-Michel. The walls consisted of smooth grey stones and mortar, some obviously showing the decades of weathering and others a little brighter and newer. Allied shelling and the Germans' return fire damaged this sanctuary, but thankfully not to the point of ruins. I stood in the square's center and looked up at the clear, blue sky turning as I looked at the church's bell tower and nearby trees. Then I realized that next to me silently stood Russ and our friends Ken, Todd, and Dave. We were all doing the same thing: slowly turning in a circle, head bent back and gazing up at the open sky. What was it really like to parachute into the darkness, not knowing where you were going to land, be it soft ground, swampy marsh, or stony street? How helpless it must have felt floating to the ground while Germans fire upon you.

My gaze landed on the church's bell tower. Fluttering in the coastal breeze was a white silk parachute hooked onto the gargoyles and adornments along the roof line. From the parachute was a suspended paratrooper—a dummy paratrooper placed there in memory of one such soldier who landed on that exact spot with his parachute tangled on the bell tower. There he hung while listening to the exchange of rifle fire between his comrades and the Germans while the town was set ablaze. Germans were directly next to him but inside the steeple shooting down at the Allied troops landing in and crossing the square. I am awed at this scene some forty-five years after it really happened. What bravery that I do not possess.

Still silent, we strolled inside the parish. The church's interior was free of ornate embellishments. Its simplicity only accentuated the beautiful stained glass window, which took the place of the customary rose window at the nave's end. The tall arched window served as a memorial to the 82nd Airborne Division and the 101st Airborne Division's paratroopers. In the window's center was the haloed Mother Mary holding a baby Jesus. On either side were two paratroopers holding on to the chute's risers with bent knees and open canopies. In the background were more tiny parachutes stacked one behind the other in golden yellows, deep blues, and vibrant reds. The bravery of the paratrooper and the Allied liberation of this town obviously were central to their present-day existence.

Opposite the church was the Airborne Museum in Sainte-Mere-Eglise, the first of several we toured over the next two days. This expansive museum proved to be my favorite. Buildings were shaped like open silk parachute canopies. The memorabilia and artifacts were fascinating. Period uniforms were on display as well as weapons, artillery, equipment, vehicles, and even a glider plane itself. I think the testimonies were the most intriguing, and I read many of them written by civilians and military alike. Everything honored the 82nd and 101st Airborne Divisions.

We emerged from the museum two hours later to stroll the streets before returning to the bus. While walking Ken called out "Bon jour" to an older gentleman of sixty years or so sitting outside a shop. The Frenchman nodded, rose to his feet, and disappeared inside the shop only to promptly return with a bottle of French wine. The man stopped beside us and looked at Russ, Ken, Todd, and Dave with their military haircuts and American garb. He spoke in English with a thick French accent, "You are Americans. Thank you," and handed Ken the bottle of wine. His eyes said more than the words expressed. The men smiled and exchanged handshakes.

It was not even midday and I felt emotionally drained from the power of Sainte-Mere-Eglise. We drove through the countryside where our next stops were Pointe du Hoc, Utah Beach, and Omaha Beach. We walked along Utah Beach near Saint Marie du Mont. The beach was so peaceful. The blues in the English Channel reminded me of the Caribbean Sea. The nearby rocks were black and jagged. From there, our tour took us to Saint Come du Mont and through the intersection now known as "Dead Man's Corner" where the roads from Utah Beach, Sainte-Mere-Eglise, and Carentan meet. We traveled along the "Purple Heart Lane," or the road leading to Carentan. We stopped briefly in Carentan and stood in the town's central square where 8th Corps commander General Troy Middleton awarded ten of the 101st Airborne Division soldiers the Silver Star. Here, the countryside has changed. The land was flat lowlands with marshes and dry land. Areas were divided by hedgerows and trees. The road was higher than the neighboring land with rocky shoulders falling away to rough vegetation. The wind blew in strong gusts across the flat land. It was obvious how easily the 101st soldiers became sitting targets on their push to Carentan. God bless every one of them.

In the evening in the hotel's garden, we gazed to the night sky and toasted the American paratroopers with French wine from a thankful gentleman.

result was missed drop zones. Some paratroopers of the 101st landed on solid pasture, which was the preference, while others found themselves in the English Channel itself, hung in trees, perched on rooftops, and mired in coastal swamps. The division was scattered all over Normandy, which confused the Germans as much as the Americans. By the evening of June 6, only one in three soldiers had found his unit.

By the time paratroopers were on the ground, 1,500 of the original 6,600 had been either killed or captured. Many were killed before they hit the ground by Germans firing into the night sky. Approximately 60 percent of their equipment was dropped into swamps or enemy hands. Some thirty-eight of the C-47 troop carriers crashed during the parachute drops, and six of those crashes took the lives of all on board.

Proud and driven, the remaining paratroopers rallied around leaders or formed small, ad-hoc units and carried out their objectives. Lieutenant Colonel Robert G. Cole, commander of the 3rd Battalion, 502nd PIR, scraped together a force of approximately seventy-five men from his own unit and other units. They marched for the northern exits from Utah Beach. Upon reaching the town of St. Martin de Varreville, Cole split his force to seize the two exits from Utah, and the men dug in to wait for the 4th Infantry Division.

South of Cole's men, Lieutenant Colonel Patrick Cassidy was rallying his men from 1st Battalion, 502nd PIR, along with an assortment of other men who had been separated from their units. Cassidy's men reinforced the northern exits from Utah Beach. Even farther to the south, the 1st and 2nd Battalions of the 506th PIR were moving through several small villages and fighting through the night. With the arriving 4th Infantry Division, the 506th PIR forces secured the southern exits from the beach front.

World War II
Medal of Honor Citation

Robert G. Cole

Rank and organization: Lieutenant Colonel, U.S. Army, 101st Airborne Division.
Place and date: Near Carentan, France, 11 June 1944.
Entered service at: San Antonio, Tex.
Birth: Fort Sam Houston, Tex.
G.O. No.: 79, 4 October 1944.
Citation: For gallantry and intrepidity at the risk of his own life, above and beyond the call of duty on 11 June 1944, in France. Lieutenant Colonel Cole was personally leading his battalion in forcing the last 4 bridges on the road to Carentan when his entire unit was suddenly pinned to the ground by intense and withering enemy rifle, machine gun, mortar, and artillery fire placed upon them from well-prepared and heavily fortified positions within 150 yards of the foremost elements. After the devastating and unceasing enemy fire had for over 1 hour prevented any move and inflicted numerous casualties, Lt. Col. Cole, observing this almost hopeless situation, courageously issued orders to assault the enemy positions with fixed bayonets. With utter disregard for his own safety and completely ignoring the enemy fire, he rose to his feet in front of his battalion and with drawn pistol shouted to his men to follow him in the assault. Catching up a fallen man's rifle and bayonet, he charged on and led the remnants of his battalion across the bullet-swept open ground and into the enemy position. His heroic and valiant action in so inspiring his men resulted in the complete establishment of our bridgehead across the Douve River. The cool fearlessness, personal bravery, and outstanding leadership displayed by Lieutenant Colonel Cole reflect great credit upon himself and are worthy of the highest praise in the military service.

Causeway to Carentan

Rallied and regrouped, and with Utah Beach secured, the 101st received new orders the following day. The V Corps had landed on Omaha Beach to the south of Utah Beach and was unable to break through and exit the beach. The 101st mission was to break through the enemy's southern flank, seize the town of Carentan between Omaha and Utah, and create a solidified link of Allied forces from Utah to Omaha beaches. The 1st and 2nd Battalions of the 506th PIR, the 3rd Battalion of the 502nd PIR, and the 1st Battalion of the 401st GIR were assigned this mission. They were later reinforced by the 327th GIR.

The ancient farming town of Carentan sat amid an array of winding rivers and saturated marshes. Several of the bridges and roadways leading to Carentan had been destroyed, and only one causeway was completely intact; the critical Carentan Causeway, or Highway N13, needed to be secured and kept passable. The onslaught of artillery from Allied ships in the English Channel in combination with German implanted explosives destroyed bridges and thoroughfares. The German forces' 6th Parachute Regiment had explicit orders from field marshal Erwin Rommel to defend Carentan to the last man. The regiment's commander, Colonel Friedrich von der Heydte, dug in his defenses between the town's boundary on the northeast and the bridge crossing the Madeleine River on Highway N13. The Germans placed a metal and concrete "Belgian gate" roadblock at the bridge. The colonel also deployed troops to

The pilot of a C-47 cargo transport crash lands safely after having dropped supplies to elements of the 101st Airborne Division which has successfully repulsed all attempts to capture the besieged city of Bastogne, Belgium, December 30, 1944. *U.S. Army photo*

Above and left: C-47s of the 101st Airborne Division drop supplies on the 4th Infantry Division Sector. This became necessary when rains and early thaw made roads impassable in this area. The supplies consisted of rations, gas, and ammunition, February 13, 1945. *U.S. Army photos*

positions in the nearby swampy fields with little dry land and cover. The causeway immediately leading to Carentan was solid, dry, and elevated above the surrounding low-lying mire. The road offered no means of concealment.

Soldiers from the 3rd Battalion, 502nd PIR, under the command of Lieutenant Colonel Cole, made their way across the Jordan River, the Douve River, and a smaller stream called le Groult. On the road nearing Carentan, the German artillery rained down on them. Snipers caught them like sitting ducks. The solid soil made digging for cover impossible. Inch by inch, the paratroopers crawled forward, many times over or around their dead comrades, who lined the road's embankment. Soldiers were pinned down and strung along the road. Once darkness fell, a German Stuka dive-bomber and other enemy planes flew at treetop level along Highway N13. They unloaded bombs and tracer rounds on the American paratroopers.

One by one, the surviving soldiers from 502nd slipped through the Madeleine River's Belgian gate under the cover of predawn's darkness on June 11, 1944. The skeletal force crossed the Madeleine River without a casualty. The lead scouts crept across flat fields to a line of hedgerows and four stone farm buildings belonging to the Ingouf family. As they neared the farmhouse, gunfire from the Germans erupted. American artillery pounded the farm buildings to no avail. The Germans answered with even heavier artillery fire. Dawn arrived, artillery smoke disseminated, and the whistle sounded. Cole shouted the order to fix bayonets and charge. Adrenaline-charged soldiers screamed like wild animals as they ran into the Germans' rifle fire. Men of the 502nd pressed forward, returning fire. The fighting at the Ingouf farm continued for the rest of the day. Soldiers from Lieutenant Colonel Cassidy's 1st Battalion, 502nd PIR, reinforced the shredded 3rd Battalion of their regiment. Reinforcements occupied positions along the road later dubbed the Cabbage Patch. A bitter close-quarters battle ensued. Germans advanced to a hedgerow closest to the farmhouse Cole was using as a command post. After finally establishing communication with an artillery liaison officer, Captain Julian Rosemund in St.-Come-du-Mont, artillery support pounded the Germans with such magnitude that the fight ended within minutes.

Meanwhile, the 327th GIR and 1st Battalion, 401st GIR, had moved south of Carentan, secured the eastern road exits from the town, and began their assault. The town was surrounded, but the Germans held on. American forces were ordered to pull back, and a massive onslaught of artillery and naval gunfire descended upon the French town. In the early morning of June 12, the bombardment was lifted, and ground forces pursued quick control. The 1st and 2nd Battalions of the 506th PIR attacked Carentan from the west, and the 501st PIR and 327th GIR attacked from the east and north. Carentan was seized.

From the 700 men under Cole's command, only 132 were left standing at the seizure of Carentan. It is said that the water along the causeway ran red with the blood of the wounded and dead Americans. The Ingoufs' farm was littered with the bodies of German and American soldiers. Under intense enemy machine-gun and artillery fire, the 3rd Battalion, 502nd PIR, men fought intently for two days before they could enter the town. The road to Carentan rightfully earned the title of "Purple Heart Lane." Ten members of the 101st Airborne Division were awarded the Silver Star. The VIII Army Corps commander, General Troy Middleton, pinned the awards on the soldiers in the Carentan town square despite interruptions by German artillery. Cole was awarded a Congressional Medal of Honor for his actions on June 11, 1944. Tragically, he did not live to receive the medal, as he was killed by enemy sniper fire in Holland on September 19, 1944.

The 1st Battalion, 401st GIR, held Carentan, while 1st and 2nd Battalions of the 327th GIR were sent to secure the high ground east of town and near Montmartin en Grainges. The 327th GIR troops encountered stubborn German resistance in the town of Rouxeville. After fierce fighting, the 2nd Battalion, 327th GIR, pushed through the German positions and linked up with a pocket of surrounded soldiers from the 29th Infantry Division.

On June 13, 1944, German counterattacks to regain Carentan and its area to the east were launched by the 37th and 38th SS panzer grenadier regiments of Gotz von Berlichingen (the 17th SS Division), along with the 6th Parachute Regiment. American troops held the line and attacked the 17th SS Division with such intensity that more than eight hundred Waffen SS troopers were killed.

By June 14, 1944, the 101st Airborne Division had secured Utah and Omaha beaches, linking the American forces landing at these Normandy coast beaches. Paratroopers

The 101st Airborne troops move out of Bastogne, after having been besieged there for ten days, to drive the enemy out of the surrounding district, Belgium, December 31, 1945. *U.S. Army photo*

continued to fight in France for the next three weeks, then returned to England to prepare for a new mission.

Operation Market Garden

The Allied forces had left plentiful supplies stranded in England, because there were not enough secured port facilities to unload them in France. Furthermore, the Allied forces needed to advance east toward Germany. So the port of Antwerp, Belgium, was the target of the 101st Airborne's next mission. The 101st Airborne Division, 82nd Airborne Division, and British 1st Airborne Division—a total of

twenty thousand soldiers—would conduct an air-drop assault on the nearby Maas, Wahl, and lower Rhine rivers. The 101st Airborne Division's mission: to jump behind enemy lines and seize some fifteen miles of highway, nicknamed "Hell's Highway," running north to the Rhine River. The British 2nd Army would launch a ground attack on the German-occupied Antwerp. On September 17, 1944, Operation Market Garden was underway.

The previously deployed pathfinder teams had laid out the drop zones with perfection. The initial daytime airborne drops were an astounding success, as the pilots did not face the challenges they did on the D-day drop. The German forces were attacked by surprise, but counterattacked with two panzer divisions in the city of Best. The 327th and 401st GIRs had landed about six hundred of their gliders containing the great majority of their equipment and heavy weapons in addition to troops. With this powerful reinforcement, the German panzers were quickly destroyed. Allied paratroopers advanced to the Maas and Wahl rivers and secured bridges across both, paving the way to Germany. After two days of action, the Allied forces pushed fifty miles into Germany. The 101st was relieved by a British armored division.

The 101st soldiers were ordered to protect the southern end of the highway and keep it from being cut off. These men bravely fought in the streets of several Dutch towns to liberate them from German control. German counterattacks were refuted with a vengeance. Meanwhile, the American 82nd Airborne, British 1st Airborne Division, and British 2nd Army continued their assault on Antwerp. The prized port city of Antwerp was in Allied forces' control, and the first supply ship from England dropped anchor on November 28, 1944. However, there was to be no rest for the weary, no time for the 101st Airborne Division to rest on their laurels.

The Battle of the Bulge (Bastogne)

The Belgian countryside was readying for the Christmas season when the Germans launched an offensive of thirteen divisions on December 16, 1944. The town of Bastogne, Belgium, situated at a junction of highways leading west into Allied-occupied France, was strategically desirable to the Germans. Their objective was to capture Bastogne and the Ardennes forest region of northern France and Belgium, retake Antwerp and its strategic port, and confine the Allied forces in the west. Their formidable force totaled two hundred fifty thousand soldiers and a thousand tanks.

The Germans were quite successful in their initial attacks and weakened the VIII Corps roadblocks positioned east of Bastogne. The Germans forcibly entered the territory, and the Allied front lines began collapsing. A quick response was needed, and men of the 101st Airborne Division were called to duty. Their mission: hold Bastogne. It was December 17, 1944.

Brigadier General Anthony McAuliffe was the 101st Airborne Division's acting commander in Europe, as Major General Maxwell D. Taylor was in Washington, D.C., at the War Department. With men tightly squeezed into trucks and trailers, McAuliffe himself led his troops over the 107 miles of frozen French land to Bastogne. American armored troops were holding their designated roadblock positions outside the town. The Germans were already there, believed to have taken up positions between these roadblocks and the Bastogne city limits. Upon the 101st Division's arrival, McAuliffe ordered Lieutenant Colonel Julian J. Ewell, commander of the 501st PIR, to conduct a diversionary attack east of Bastogne to distract the Germans from the city. The operation worked perfectly, and the 101st Division drove the remaining Germans from Bastogne's immediate area to establish a firm hold on the city and its perimeter.

The Germans, now outside the city and desperately wanting it, completely surrounded the 101st Airborne Division with elements of their 10th Armored Division. The 101st Airborne's contact with Allied forces and supplies had been severed. The division was without winter clothes suitable for the harsh, bitter weather. The German attacks were brutal and intense. Artillery pounded the American troops, but they fiercely held Bastogne. Many times they were engaged in hand-to-hand and close-quarters combat in such neighboring villages as Neffe, Marvie, and Champs. On December 22, 1944, the German commander offered his terms of surrender, to which McAuliffe issued the brief decline, "Nuts!" The German divisions launched siege after siege and attack after attack, but the 101st held on tight.

Four days later, on December 26, 1944, deliverance came. The 326th Airborne Engineers reported contact with "three light tanks believed friendly." And they were. The U.S. Army 4th Armored Division broke through the German lines and reinforced the battered American troops in Bastogne. The frozen and famished troops received air-dropped supplies and artillery support. Several cargo gliders landed and delivered much-needed medical personnel and equipment for the wounded. With the arrival of General George S. Patton's 3rd Army, the 101st and its reinforcements began to attack the Germans surrounding the city.

On December 26, 1944, the Siege of Bastogne could be considered finished; however, the fight was not over. The Germans are not willing to give up their mission and launched attack after attack. For the following three weeks, American forces fought relentlessly. The Germans were finally driven out of Belgian countryside and back into Germany itself. On January 18, 1945, the 101st Airborne Division at Bastogne was relieved by the VII Corps.

Unfortunately, a casualty roster of the units fighting east of Bastogne prior to December 19 could not be accurately gathered, according to the Department of the Army's Office of the Chief of Military History. Similarly, there is no means of numbering the killed, wounded, and missing in the mixture of unrecorded tankers, gunners, infantrymen, and others who courageously fought in the defense of Bastogne. The 101st Airborne Division recorded 105 officers and 1,536 enlisted men as battle casualties. Among them was the 501st PIR's commander, Lieutenant Colonel Ewell.

The Close of World War II

After Bastogne, the 101st Airborne Division moved to Drulingen and Pfaffenhoffen in the French region of Alsace and engaged in defensive patrols along the Moder River. The unit assembled in Mourmelon, France, for additional training before moving to the Ruhr region of Germany at the end of March 1945.

With springtime came a new mission for the 101st Airborne Division. In April 1945, the 101st teamed with the 3rd Infantry Division in an assault on Adolf Hitler's mountain retreat on the Obersalzberg, located in southeastern Bavaria just in the mountains two miles east and 1,200 feet above the quiet Alpine town of Berchtesgaden. Over the years and under the direction of Reichsleiter Martin Bormann, the Obersalzberg had evolved into an expansive complex with homes for the Nazi hierarchy, such as Reichsmarschall Hermann Göring, chief of the German air force, and Bormann himself. SS troop barracks, tunnel and bunker complexes, rail lines, and support facilities for workers and their families absorbed the mountain top. The famed Kehlsteinhaus (a.k.a. the Eagle's Nest) was poised at an even higher elevation on the Hoher Göll mountain.

This Alpine area was the target for the British Royal Air Force bombing raids on April 25, 1945, which successfully

World War II
Medal of Honor Citation

Joe E. Mann

Rank and organization: Private First Class, U.S. Army, Company H, 502d Parachute Infantry, 101st Airborne Division.

Place and date: Best, Holland, 18 September 1944.

Entered service at: Seattle, Wash.

Birth: Rearden, Wash.

G.O. No.: 73, 30 August 1945.

Citation: He distinguished himself by conspicuous gallantry above and beyond the call of duty. On 18 September 1944, in the vicinity of Best, Holland, his platoon, attempting to seize the bridge across the Wilhelmina Canal, was surrounded and isolated by an enemy force greatly superior in personnel and firepower. Acting as lead scout, Pfc. Mann boldly crept to within rocket-launcher range of an enemy artillery position and, in

the face of heavy enemy fire, destroyed an 88mm gun and an ammunition dump. Completely disregarding the great danger involved, he remained in his exposed position, and, with his M-1 rifle, killed the enemy one by one until he was wounded four times. Taken to a covered position, he insisted on returning to a forward position to stand guard during the night. On the following morning the enemy launched a concerted attack and advanced to within a few yards of the position, throwing hand grenades as they approached. One of these landed within a few feet of Private First Class Mann. Unable to raise his arms, which were bandaged to his body, he yelled "grenade" and threw his body over the grenade, and as it exploded, died. His outstanding gallantry above and beyond the call of duty and his magnificent conduct were an everlasting inspiration to his comrades for whom he gave his life.

destroyed many of the buildings. The remains of Hitler's home, Berghof, were set on fire by departing SS troops on May 4, 1945. The smoldering ruins were found by the U.S. Army's 3rd Infantry Division that same day. Some accounts say the 3rd Infantry Division were the first Allied troops to arrive on the Obersalzberg. Other accounts indicate that the French 2nd Armored Division first secured the Eagle's Nest and were followed by men of the 1st Battalion, 506th PIR, close thereafter.

It was in the historic French city of Reims, east of Paris, that the German general Alfred Jodl signed the unconditional surrender of all German forces on all fighting fronts, the first of two documents that ended the European theater of operations in World War II. The time was 2:41 a.m. on May 7, 1945.

In the pictorial Bavarian region, the 101st Airborne Division accepted the surrender of the German XII SS and LXXXII Corps. Colonel Robert Sink, commander of the 506th PIR, accepted the surrender of *Generalleutnant* Theodor Tolsdorff, commander of the German LXXXII Corps near Stockklaus, Austria, effective May 8, 1945. The 101st Airborne hunted down and captured key members of the Nazi regime who had gone into hiding. These individuals were later brought before the War Crimes Tribunal at The Hague. The 506th PIR captured *Generalfeldmarschall* Albert Kesselring, commander in chief of the Nazi party. The 502nd PIR

captured Julius Streicher, editor of *Der Sturmer*, a German weekly newspaper that published anti-Semitic propaganda. *Obergruppenfuhrer* Karl Oberg, the chief of German SS in occupied France, and *Generaloberst* (Colonel General) Heinz Guderian, a leading armor expert, were also captured by the 502nd PIR. The troops of the 101st Division also removed Göring's priceless art treasures, many taken from the Berlin museum and valued at $500 million, from a private train to a building in Unterstein.

The 101st Airborne Division remained in Berchtesgaden area and in parts of Austria until ordered to Auxerre, France, to begin training for the invasion of Japan. But Japan's surrender on September 2, 1945, made the unit's deployment to the Pacific unnecessary, and the 101st Airborne Division was deactivated on November 30, 1945, in Auxerre.

During World War II, the 101st Airborne Division spent 214 days in combat. Medals of Honor were awarded to 101st Airborne Division soldiers Lieutenant Colonel Robert G. Cole and Private First Class Joe E. Mann for their gallantry above and beyond the call of duty. Men of the 101st Airborne Division were awarded 47 Distinguished Service Crosses, 516 Silver Stars, and 6,977 Bronze Stars. The division was responsible for capturing 29,527 enemy soldiers. With victories come deep and poignant sacrifices. In the 101st Airborne Division, 2,043 soldiers were killed in action, 7,976 were wounded, 1,193 were missing in action, and 336 were taken prisoner.

Chapter 3

THE SCREAMING EAGLES IN VIETNAM

3rd Battalion, 502nd Infantry Regiment: A Proud Legacy Continues

The 3rd Battalion, 502nd Infantry Regiment, was assigned to the 101st Airborne Division in June 1984. Within the next month, the unit was deployed to Sinai, Egypt, as part of the Multinational Forces and Observers' mission to implement the security provisions outlined in the 1979 Israeli-Egypt peace treaty. As a result of their professionalism and outstanding service, soldiers of the 3rd Battalion earned a Superior Unit Award for their quick action to prevent a terrorist act from reigniting hostilities between Egypt and Israel. This award was the first of its kind in the U.S. Army. On December 12, 1985, while en route to Fort Campbell, Kentucky, their charter aircraft crashed shortly after its take-off from Gander International Airport in Newfoundland, Canada. An explosive post-crash fire and the rugged terrain made rescue efforts futile, and 248 of the 3rd Battalion, 502nd Infantry Regiment, 101st Airborne Division, soldiers tragically perished.

In August 1990, the soldiers of the 3rd Battalion, 502nd Infantry Regiment, led the 101st Division's deployment to Saudi Arabia for Operation Desert Shield. In combat operations against Iraq, 3rd Battalion soldiers exhibited their proud legacy as they participated in the largest helicopter assault in history to defeat retreating Iraqi forces in the Euphrates Valley.

Soldiers of the 502nd Infantry Regiment have also participated in peace-keeping and contingency operations. In 1993 and 1994, soldiers of 1st and 3rd Battalions deployed to the Republic of Panama to assist in the repatriation of Cuban refugees.

On January 15, 1995, 3rd Battalion, 502nd Infantry, was deployed to Panama as part of Operation Safe Passage. Led by commander Lieutenant Colonel Ben F. Clawson, 3rd Battalion's mission was to transport Cuban migrants from Operation Safe Haven camps to Howard Air Force Base. From there, the Cubans would travel to the secure Guantanamo Bay, Cuba. After the mission's successful completion, 3rd Battalion returned to Fort Campbell, Kentucky, on February 23, 1995.

In May 1954, the 101st Airborne Division had been designated as a training unit at Fort Jackson, South Carolina. In 1956, the division was moved to Fort Campbell, Kentucky, and reorganized as a combat division. On September 21, 1956, the unit was formally moved to Fort Campbell, Kentucky, and returned to active duty status. The 101st was called to suppress major civil disturbances at Little Rock, Arkansas, in 1957; Oxford, Mississippi, in 1962; and Detroit, Michigan, in 1967. Meanwhile, in the early 1960s, the U.S. Army predicted its increased involvement in Southeast Asia and began building the 101st Airborne Division's strength and numbers. In the meantime, the division was used to test new equipment and operational concepts, including survival skills on a nuclear battlefield.

On July 28, 1965, President Lyndon B. Johnson announced his plans to increase American military strength in South Vietnam. The newly activated 1st Cavalry Division (Airmobile), with its large contingency of helicopters, and all three brigades of the 1st Infantry Division were deployed to South Vietnam. The 101st Airborne Division received orders for combat in Vietnam in July 1965. Hundreds of support and logistical units were sent to Southeast Asia as well. Deployment of these combat units to the region increased the U.S. military strength from approximately fifty thousand to one hundred seventy-five thousand troops during the following six months.

The original 101st Airborne Division had included nothing but airborne-qualified personnel among its ranks. In 1943, while training in England, the 101st Airborne Division

Private First Class John Henson of the 1st Battalion, 327th Infantry, 101st Airborne Division, cleans his M-16 rifle while on an operation thirty miles west of Kontum, July 12, 1966. *U.S. Army photo*

had realized the need for airborne-qualified support personnel and began training all its infantrymen and support personnel to be paratroopers. Twenty-five years later, in the jungles of Southeast Asia, the combat situation in Vietnam changed the formation and composition for the 101st Division again.

The standard tactical advantages of paratroopers were not readily applicable to this new battle front. Additionally, the casualty rate and concluding tours of duty caused a shortage of airborne-qualified soldiers, and there weren't enough new paratroopers to meet the division's demands. Thus, in spring of 1968, the 101st Airborne Division added "legs" to their ranks—infantrymen who were not parachutists. Patterning itself after the 1st Air Cavalry Division, the 101st Airborne Division adopted tactical operations utilizing the air mobility of the helicopter. To reflect these new modern tactics, yet maintain its heritage, the 101st Airborne Division's name was modified to 101st Airborne Division (Airmobile).

Opening Operations

The 101st Airborne Division's 1st Brigade landed at Cam Ranh Bay in South Vietnam on July 29, 1965. The 1st Brigade comprised the 1st and 2nd Battalions of the 327th Infantry and 2nd Battalion of the 502nd Infantry. Almost immediately after their arrival, the 1st Brigade was ordered into the Song Con Valley, which lay about twenty miles northeast of the town of An Khe.

Fighting was intense and deadly. During one particular mission, 1st Battalion, 327th Infantry, encountered heavy enemy fire at its landing zone. Enemy contact was so close that air support and artillery strikes could not be called in. Many American losses were incurred, including three company commanders. Finally, 1st Battalion was able to pull back, and air strikes on North Vietnamese forces ensued. After bombarding enemy forces at night with approximately a hundred sorties and eleven thousand rounds of ammunition, the men of 101st Airborne were extracted by helicopter. Only then did they realize they had previously landed in the middle of a heavily entrenched North Vietnamese military base.

The North Vietnamese Army (NVA) had mounted an offensive in South Vietnam's Central Highlands. As communist forces attacked border camps and civilian villages and towns, airmobile units such as the 1st Air Cavalry and 101st Airborne Division were called to the area. During the remainder of 1965, the 1st Brigade of the 101st Airborne Division continued patrols and disrupted enemy supply lines.

By early 1966, the constant patrols led to a reduction in enemy operations in the area, but the enemy had not given up. The NWA began to build up its forces in the Pleiku and Kontum provinces. In the northern South Vietnamese base camp of Dak To, South Vietnamese forces were surrounded by the 24th NVA Regiment, and the 1st Brigade of the 101st Airborne Division was sent to reinforce the South Vietnamese position.

When the 101st Airborne Division arrived, the exhausted South Vietnamese forces were evacuated immediately from the Dak To base camp. The 101st Division's 2nd Battalion, 502nd Infantry, dug in and established its defensive positions inside the now-abandoned camp. Company C was sent to a forward, exposed defensive position. During the night of June 6, 1966, the 24th NVA Regiment attacked the company with intense, close-quarters fighting. In desperation, the company commander of Company C made an incredibly difficult decision: he called in air strikes on top of his own position, killing both enemy NVA and American soldiers. As a result, the 24th NVA Regiment pulled back. Helicopters rapidly transported in Company A of the 1st Battalion, 327th Infantry, to reinforce Company C's positions, and American forces pursued the retreating North Vietnamese troops. Several large-scale air attacks were dropped on the enemy force, killing hundreds of North Vietnamese soldiers. However, the 24th NVA somehow escaped into Laos.

Over the following two years, the 1st Brigade of the 101st Airborne Division acted as a ready reaction force to reinforce various contingencies of American and South Vietnamese forces. The unit was airlifted and dropped into positions throughout the Kontum province, Quang Tri province, and others to block the Vietnamese enemy forces retreating into Laos, conduct lengthy ground patrols, and reinforce American units under attack. As a result, the troops of the 1st Brigade honed their ability to execute rapid helicopter assaults.

In April 1967, the 1st Brigade was temporarily placed under the operational control of the 3rd Marine Amphibious Force as part of Task Force Oregon. In the Quang Tri province, the 1st Brigade participated in a large-scale effort to push the North Vietnamese from the villages. In the fall of 1967, Task Force Oregon was reorganized and reassigned to the 23rd Infantry Division. The 1st Brigade of the 101st Airborne Division was detached from this mission and instructed to wait for the arrival of the 2nd and 3rd Brigades of the 101st Airborne Division; the three brigades united in December 1967 in time for the new year.

Têt Nguyên Dán, or Feast of the First Morning, is more commonly known by its abbreviated name Têt. Falling at the end of January and lasting three days, the Têt is a traditional new year celebration that is considered the most important public holiday in Vietnam. Customarily, the Vietnamese people prepare elaborate holiday foods, celebrate with their families, and visit the temples. It is a time to forget about the troubles of the past year and hope for a better future. The Têt was supposed to be a peaceful time, but in 1968 it was anything but. On January 31, 1968, the North Vietnamese Army launched an offensive attack that caught the American forces completely by surprise.

Increased truck movements along the Ho Chi Minh Trail and a buildup of NVA troops signaled to U.S. military intelligence that a North Vietnamese offensive action was looming. But because North Vietnam had announced in October 1967 that it would observe a seven-day truce from January 27 to February 3, 1968, in honor of Têt, South Vietnam and the United States were unprepared for an attack. The Tet Offensive was timed to begin on the night of January 30–31, 1968. Battalion-strength elements of the People's Liberation Armed Forces of the National Liberation Front (NLF), or the Viet Cong, and division-strength elements of the NVA simultaneously launched an offensive action on a national scale, aiming numerous direct assaults at major cities and towns.

The ancient city of Hue's locale placed it close to both the South Vietnam and North Vietnam borders, although technically located in South Vietnam. The North Vietnamese believed that Hue should be their first political stronghold in the South due to its communist ties and history of Buddhist activism. Regular North Vietnamese forces were sent to capture the city, which was defended by South Vietnamese Army (SVA) units. The North Vietnamese quickly drove the South Vietnamese from Hue.

The 101st Airborne Division and 1st Calvary Division were sent to recapture the city, and an intense battle raged in Hu? for more than three weeks. Advances were measured house by house, and each dwelling seemed to hold more enemy soldiers. The 5th Marine Regiment was called in to reinforce American troops. American firepower from the ground, nearby U.S. naval ships, and bombing runs destroyed much of the city and its historical buildings. Hue was finally liberated from North Vietnamese control by U.S., South Vietnamese, and allied forces, but not without significant human costs. During the Tet Offensive, thousands of enemy soldiers were killed and thousands more were captured. The years that have followed reveal the inhumane atrocities, such as imprisonment, torture, and executions that the North Vietnamese and Viet Cong wielded upon the Vietnamese people, American civilians, and American service members in the city of Hue.

Nationwide, the Tet Offensive continued until July 1969. The 101st Airborne Division had its resources and manpower divided between defending the city of Hue and executing operations in other enemy-controlled territory. In the coastal region of the Thua Thlen province, the 101st participated in Operation Nevada Eagle and captured supplies. The division's patrols and raids cleared the land of enemy forces, and the unit captured enough rice, weapons, and equipment for ten enemy battalions. When the NVA re-established their stocks of rice, ammunition, and equipment in South Vietnam's A Shau Valley, the 101st launched air assaults, established fire-support bases, and raided the lowlands and surrounding hills to locate enemy forces and supplies. For 288 days, the 101st attacked and captured enemy supply bases in the valley during Operation Somerset Plain.

The 28th NVA Regiment had dug into a particular A Shau Valley hillside in tiers of fortified bunkers and were waiting for the U.S. forces to attack. At 937 meters above sea level, Hill 937, locally known as the Dong Ap Bia Mountain, dominated the surrounding hilltops. The area was enveloped by triple-canopied tropical vegetation, dense bamboo, and razor-sharp elephant grass. Hill 937, later called "Hamburger Hill," became the target for Operation Apache Snow, scheduled for May 10, 1969. Eighteen hundred men from three airmobile infantry battalions of the 101st Airborne Division's 3rd Brigade (1st Battalion of the 506th Infantry, 2nd Battalion of the 501st Infantry, and 3rd Battalion of the 187th Infantry) and two battalions of the South Vietnamese Army's 1st Division were assembled for the largest airmobile assault of the Vietnam War.

Helicopter pilots and their door gunners had prepared their aircraft. Artillery batteries at nearby fire bases were poised and ready.

Determined to hold their position, the North Vietnamese regiment strongly resisted the U.S. and South Vietnamese forces. For ten days, fierce battles ensued, involving artillery bombardments, air strikes, and hand-to-hand combat. Eventually, the five airmobile infantry battalions, ten artillery batteries, 450 tons of bombs, and 69 tons of napalm devastated and captured the hillside. Reports indicated American losses at 70 dead and 372 wounded. The number of enemy losses could not be accurate, as 630 perished on the battlefield with more already buried in underground mortuaries. The A Shau Valley was finally

Vietnam War: Medal of Honor Citation

Webster Anderson

Rank and organization: Sergeant First Class, U.S. Army, Battery A, 2d Battalion, 320th Field Artillery, 101st Airborne Infantry Division (Airmobile).
Place and date: Tam Ky, Republic of Vietnam, 15 October 1967.
Entered service at: Winnsboro, S.C.
Born: 15 July 1933, Winnsboro, S.C.
Citation: Sfc. Anderson (then S/Sgt.), distinguished himself by conspicuous gallantry and intrepidity in action while serving as chief of section in Battery A, against a hostile force. During the early morning hours Battery A's defensive position was attacked by a determined North Vietnamese Army infantry unit supported by heavy mortar, recoilless rifle, rocket propelled grenade and automatic weapon fire. The initial enemy onslaught breached the battery defensive perimeter. Sfc. Anderson, with complete disregard for his personal safety, mounted the exposed parapet of his howitzer position and became the mainstay of the defense of the battery position. Sfc. Anderson directed devastating direct howitzer fire on the assaulting enemy while providing rifle and grenade defensive fire against enemy soldiers attempting to overrun his gun section position. While protecting his crew and directing their fire against the enemy from his exposed position, 2 enemy grenades exploded at his feet knocking him down and severely wounding him in the legs. Despite the excruciating pain and though not able to stand, Sfc. Anderson valorously propped himself on the parapet and continued to

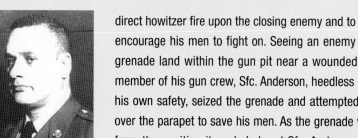

direct howitzer fire upon the closing enemy and to encourage his men to fight on. Seeing an enemy grenade land within the gun pit near a wounded member of his gun crew, Sfc. Anderson, heedless of his own safety, seized the grenade and attempted to throw it over the parapet to save his men. As the grenade was thrown from the position it exploded and Sfc. Anderson was again grievously wounded. Although only partially conscious and severely wounded, Sfc. Anderson refused medical evacuation and continued to encourage his men in the defense of the position. Sfc. Anderson by his inspirational leadership, professionalism, devotion to duty and complete disregard for his welfare was able to maintain the defense of his section position and to defeat a determined attack. Sfc. Anderson's gallantry and extraordinary heroism at the risk of his life above and beyond the call of duty are in the highest traditions of the military service and reflect great credit upon himself, his unit, and the U.S. Army.

Paul William Bucha

Rank and organization: Captain, U.S. Army, Company D, 3d Battalion. 187th Infantry, 3d Brigade, 101st Airborne Division.
Place and date: Near Phuoc Vinh, Binh Duong Province, Republic of Vietnam, 16–19 March 1968.
Entered service at: U.S. Military Academy, West Point, N.Y.

cleared of enemy forces, and the U.S. armored forces were brought in to re-establish airstrips.

Following these operations, the 101st Airborne Division was reorganized, and its name was changed to the 101st Airborne Division (Airmobile). A new mission followed: "Vietnamization." The 101st Airborne Division was sent to the Thua Thlen province to participate in civil operations and train the South Vietnamese forces to fight the fight and operate on their own. In late 1971 and early 1972, the 101st Airborne Division began its return to home at Fort Campbell, Kentucky. After spending nearly seven years of combat in South Vietnam, it was the last U.S. Army division to leave.

Born: 1 August 1943, Washington, D.C.

Citation: For conspicuous gallantry and intrepidity in action at the risk of his life above and beyond the call of duty. Captain Bucha distinguished himself while serving as commanding officer, Company D, on a reconnaissance-in-force mission against enemy forces near Phuoc Vinh. The company was inserted by helicopter into the suspected enemy stronghold to locate and destroy the enemy. During this period Captain Bucha aggressively and courageously led his men in the destruction of enemy fortifications and base areas and eliminated scattered resistance impeding the advance of the company. On 18 March while advancing to contact, the lead elements of the company became engaged by the heavy automatic weapon, heavy machine gun, rocket propelled grenade, Claymore mine and small-arms fire of an estimated battalion-size force. Captain Bucha, with complete disregard for his safety, moved to the threatened area to direct the defense and ordered reinforcements to the aid of the lead element. Seeing that his men were pinned down by heavy machine-gun fire from a concealed bunker located some 40 meters to the front of the positions, Captain Bucha crawled through the hail of fire to single-handedly destroy the bunker with grenades. During this heroic action Captain Bucha received a painful shrapnel wound. Returning to the perimeter, he observed that his unit could not hold its positions and repel the human wave assaults launched by the determined enemy. Captain Bucha ordered the withdrawal of the unit elements and covered the withdrawal to positions of a company perimeter from which he could direct fire upon the charging enemy. When a friendly element retrieving casualties was ambushed and cut off from the perimeter, Captain Bucha ordered them to feign death and he directed artillery fire around them. During the night Captain Bucha moved throughout the position, distributing ammunition, providing encouragement and insuring the integrity of the defense. He directed artillery, helicopter gunship and Air Force gunship fire on the enemy strong points and attacking forces, marking the positions with smoke grenades. Using flashlights in complete view of enemy snipers, he directed the medical evacuation of 3 air-ambulance loads of seriously wounded personnel and the helicopter supply of his company. At daybreak Captain Bucha led a rescue party to recover the dead and wounded members of the ambushed element. During the period of intensive combat, Captain Bucha, by his extraordinary heroism, inspirational example, outstanding leadership and professional competence, led his company in the decimation of a superior enemy force, which left 156 dead on the battlefield. His bravery and gallantry at the risk of his life are in the highest traditions of the military service. Captain Bucha has reflected great credit on himself, his unit, and the U.S. Army.

Michael John Fitzmaurice

Rank and organization: Specialist Fourth Class, U.S. Army, Troop D, 2d Squadron, 17th Cavalry, 101st Airborne Division.

Place and date: Khe Sanh, Republic of Vietnam, 23 March 1971. Entered service at: Jamestown, N. Dak.

Born: 9 March 1950, Jamestown, N. Dak.

Citation: For conspicuous gallantry and intrepidity in action at the risk of his life above and beyond the call of duty. Sp4c.

Fitzmaurice, 3d Platoon, Troop D, distinguished himself at Khe Sanh. Sp4c. Fitzmaurice and 3 fellow soldiers were occupying a bunker when a company of North Vietnamese sappers infiltrated the area. At the onset of the attack Sp4c. Fitzmaurice observed 3 explosive charges which had been thrown into the bunker by the enemy. Realizing the imminent danger to his comrades, and with complete disregard for his personal safety, he hurled 2 of the charges out of the bunker. He then threw his flak vest and himself over the remaining charge. By this courageous act he absorbed the blast and shielded his fellow-soldiers. Although suffering from serious multiple wounds and partial loss of sight, he charged out of the bunker and engaged the enemy until his rifle was damaged by the blast of an enemy hand grenade. While in search of another weapon, Sp4c. Fitzmaurice encountered and overcame an enemy sapper in hand-to-hand combat. Having obtained another weapon, he returned to his original fighting position and inflicted additional casualties on the attacking enemy. Although seriously wounded, Sp4c. Fitzmaurice refused to be medically evacuated, preferring to remain at his post. Sp4c. Fitzmaurice's extraordinary heroism in action at the risk of his life contributed significantly to the successful defense of the position and resulted in saving the lives of a number of his fellow soldiers. These acts of heroism go above and beyond the call of duty, are in keeping with the highest traditions of the military service, and reflect great credit on Sp4c. Fitzmaurice and the U.S. Army.

Frank R. Fratellenico

Rank and organization: Corporal, U.S. Army, Company B, 2d Battalion, 502d Infantry, 1st Brigade, 101st Airborne Division.
Place and date: Quang Tri Province, Republic of Vietnam, 19 August 1970.
Entered service at: Albany, N.Y.
Born: 14 July 1951, Sharon, Conn.
Citation: Cpl. Fratellenico distinguished himself while serving as a rifleman with Company B. Cpl. Fratellenico's squad was pinned down by intensive fire from 2 well-fortified enemy bunkers. At great personal risk Cpl. Fratellenico maneuvered forward and, using hand grenades, neutralized the first bunker which was occupied by a number of enemy soldiers. While attacking the second bunker, enemy fire struck Cpl. Fratellenico, causing him to fall to the ground and drop a grenade which he was preparing to throw. Alert to the imminent danger to his comrades, Cpl. Fratellenico retrieved the grenade and fell upon it an instant before it exploded. His heroic actions prevented death or serious injury to 4 of his comrades nearby and inspired his unit which subsequently overran the enemy position. Cpl. Fratellenico's conspicuous gallantry, extraordinary heroism, and intrepidity at the cost of his life, above and beyond the call of duty, are in keeping with the highest traditions of the military service and reflect great credit on him, his unit, and the U.S. Army.

James A. Gardner

Rank and organization: First Lieutenant, U.S. Army, Headquarters and Headquarters Company, 1st Battalion (Airborne), 327th Infantry, 1st Brigade, 101st Airborne Division.
Place and date: My Canh, Vietnam, 7 February 1966.
Entered service at: Memphis, Tenn.
Born: 7 February 1943, Dyersburg, Tenn.
Citation: For conspicuous gallantry and intrepidity in action at the risk of his life above and beyond the call of duty. 1st Lt. Gardner's platoon was advancing to relieve a company of the 1st Battalion that had been pinned down for several hours by a numerically superior enemy force in the village of My Canh, Vietnam. The enemy occupied a series of strongly fortified bunker positions which were mutually supporting and expertly concealed. Approaches to the position were well covered by an integrated pattern of fire including automatic weapons, machine guns and mortars. Air strikes and artillery placed on the fortifications had little effect. 1st Lt. Gardner's platoon was to relieve the friendly company by encircling and destroying

the enemy force. Even as it moved to begin the attack, the platoon was under heavy enemy fire. During the attack, the enemy fire intensified. Leading the assault and disregarding his own safety, 1st Lt. Gardner charged through a withering hail of fire across an open rice paddy. On reaching the first bunker he destroyed it with a grenade and without hesitation dashed to the second bunker and eliminated it by tossing a grenade inside. Then, crawling swiftly along the dike of a rice paddy, he reached the third bunker. Before he could arm a grenade, the enemy gunner leaped forth, firing at him. 1st Lt. Gardner instantly returned the fire and killed the enemy gunner at a distance of 6 feet. Following the seizure of the main enemy position, he reorganized the platoon to continue the attack. Advancing to the new assault position, the platoon was pinned down by an enemy machine gun emplaced in a fortified bunker. 1st Lt. Gardner immediately collected several grenades and charged the enemy position, firing his rifle as he advanced to neutralize the defenders. He dropped a grenade into the bunker and vaulted beyond. As the bunker blew up, he came under fire again. Rolling into a ditch to gain cover, he moved toward the new source of fire. Nearing the position, he leaped from the ditch and advanced with a grenade in one hand and firing his rifle with the other. He was gravely wounded just before he reached the bunker, but with a last valiant effort he staggered forward and destroyed the bunker and its defenders with a grenade. Although he fell dead on the rim of the bunker, his extraordinary actions so inspired the men of his platoon that they resumed the attack and completely routed the enemy. 1st Lt. Gardner's conspicuous gallantry was in the highest traditions of the U.S. Army.

John G. Gertsch

Rank and organization: Staff Sergeant, U.S. Army, Company E, 1st Battalion, 327th Infantry, 101st Airborne Division.

Place and date: A Shau Valley, Republic of Vietnam, 15 to 19 July 1969.

Entered service at: Buffalo, N.Y.

Born: 29 September 1944, Jersey City, N.J.:

Citation: S/Sgt. Gertsch distinguished himself while serving as a platoon sergeant and platoon leader during combat operations in the A Shau Valley. During the initial phase of an operation to seize a strongly defended enemy position, S/Sgt. Gertsch's platoon leader was seriously wounded and lay exposed to intense enemy fire. Forsaking his own safety, without hesitation S/Sgt. Gertsch rushed to aid his fallen leader and dragged him to a sheltered position. He then assumed command of the heavily engaged platoon and led his men in a fierce counterattack that forced the enemy to withdraw. Later, a small element of S/Sgt. Gertsch's unit was reconnoitering when attacked again by the enemy. S/Sgt. Gertsch moved forward to his besieged element and immediately charged, firing as he advanced. His determined assault forced the enemy troops to withdraw in confusion and made possible the recovery of 2 wounded men who had been exposed to heavy enemy fire. Sometime later his platoon came under attack by an enemy force employing automatic weapons, grenade, and rocket fire. S/Sgt. Gertsch was severely wounded during the onslaught but continued to command his platoon despite his painful wound. While moving under fire and encouraging his men he sighted an aidman treating a wounded officer from an adjacent unit. Realizing that both men were in imminent danger of being killed, he rushed forward and positioned himself between them and the enemy nearby. While the wounded officer was being moved to safety S/Sgt. Gertsch was mortally wounded by enemy fire. Without S/Sgt. Gertsch's courage, ability to inspire others, and profound concern for the welfare of his men, the loss of life among his fellow soldiers would have been significantly greater. His conspicuous gallantry, extraordinary heroism, and intrepidity at the cost of his life, above and beyond the call of duty, are in the highest traditions of the U.S. Army and reflect great credit on him and the Armed Forces of his country.

Peter M. Guenette

Rank and organization: Specialist Fourth Class, U.S. Army, Company D, 2d Battalion (Airborne), 506th Infantry, 101st Airborne Division (Airmobile).

Place and date: Quan Tan Uyen Province, Republic of Vietnam, 18 May 1968.

Entered service at: Albany, N.Y.

Born: 4 January 1948, Troy, N.Y.

Citation: For conspicuous gallantry and intrepidity in action at the risk of his life above and beyond the call of duty. Sp4c. Guenette distinguished himself while serving as a machine gunner with Company D, during combat operations. While Sp4c. Guenette's platoon was sweeping a suspected enemy base camp, it came under light harassing fire from a well equipped and firmly entrenched squad of North Vietnamese Army regulars which was serving as a delaying force at the entrance to their base camp. As the platoon moved within 10 meters of the fortified positions, the enemy fire became intense. Sp4c. Guenette and his assistant gunner immediately began to provide a base of suppressive fire, ceasing momentarily to allow the assistant gunner time to throw a grenade into a bunker. Seconds later, an enemy grenade was thrown to Sp4c. Guenette's right flank. Realizing that the grenade would kill or wound at least 4 men and destroy the machine gun, he shouted a warning and smothered the grenade with his body, absorbing its blast. Through his actions, he prevented loss of life or injury to at least 3 men and enabled his comrades to maintain their fire superiority. By his gallantry at the cost of his life in keeping with the highest traditions of the military service, Sp4c. Guenette has reflected great credit on himself, his unit, and the U.S. Army.

Frank A. Herda

Rank and organization: Specialist Fourth Class, U.S. Army, Company A, 1st Battalion (Airborne), 506th Infantry, 101st Airborne Division (Airmobile).

Place and date: Near Dak To, Quang Trang Province, Republic of Vietnam, 29 June 1968.

Entered service at: Cleveland, Ohio.

Born: 13 September 1947, Cleveland, Ohio.

Citation: For conspicuous gallantry and intrepidity in action at the risk of his life above and beyond the call of duty. Sp4c. Herda (then Pfc.) distinguished himself while serving as a grenadier with Company A. Company A was part of a battalion-size night defensive perimeter when a large enemy force initi-

ated an attack on the friendly units. While other enemy elements provided diversionary fire and indirect weapons fire to the west, a sapper force of approximately 30 men armed with hand grenades and small charges attacked Company A's perimeter from the east. As the sappers were making a last, violent assault, 5 of them charged the position defended by Sp4c. Herda and 2 comrades, 1 of whom was wounded and lay helpless in the bottom of the foxhole. Sp4c. Herda fired at the aggressors until they were within 10 feet of his position and 1 of their grenades landed in the foxhole. He fired 1 last round from his grenade launcher, hitting 1 of the enemy soldiers in the head, and then, with no concern for his safety, Sp4c. Herda immediately covered the blast of the grenade with his body. The explosion wounded him grievously, but his selfless action prevented his 2 comrades from being seriously injured or killed and enabled the remaining defender to kill the other sappers. By his gallantry at the risk of his life in the highest traditions of the military service, Sp4c. Herda has reflected great credit on himself, his unit, and the U.S. Army.

Joe R. Hooper

Rank and organization: Staff Sergeant, U.S. Army, Company D, 2d Battalion (Airborne), 501st Infantry, 101st Airborne Division.

Place and date: Near Hue, Republic of Vietnam, 21 February 1968.

Entered service at: Los Angeles, Calif. Born: 8 August 1938, Piedmont, S.C.

Citation: For conspicuous gallantry and intrepidity in action at the risk of his life above and beyond the call of duty. Staff Sergeant (then Sgt.) Hooper, U.S. Army, distinguished himself while serving as squad leader with Company D. Company D was assaulting a heavily defended enemy position along a river bank when it encountered a withering hail of fire from rockets, machine guns and automatic weapons. S/Sgt. Hooper rallied several men and stormed across the river, overrunning several bunkers on the opposite shore. Thus inspired, the rest of the company moved to the attack. With utter disregard for his own safety, he moved out under the intense fire again and pulled back the wounded, moving them to safety. During this act S/Sgt. Hooper was seriously wounded, but he refused medical aid and returned to his men. With the relentless enemy fire disrupting the attack, he single-handedly stormed 3 enemy bunkers, destroying them with hand grenade and rifle fire, and shot 2 enemy soldiers who had attacked and wounded the Chaplain. Leading his men forward in a sweep of the area, S/Sgt. Hooper destroyed 3 buildings housing enemy riflemen. At this point he was attacked by a North Vietnamese officer whom he fatally wounded with his bayonet. Finding his men under heavy fire from a house to the front, he proceeded alone to the building, killing its occupants with rifle fire and grenades. By now his initial body wound had been compounded by grenade fragments, yet despite the multiple wounds and loss of blood, he continued to lead his men against the intense enemy fire. As his squad reached the final line of enemy resistance, it received devastating fire from 4 bunkers in line on its left flank. S/Sgt. Hooper gathered several hand grenades and raced down a small trench which ran the length of the bunker line, tossing grenades into each bunker as he passed by, killing all but 2 of the occupants. With these positions destroyed, he concentrated on the last bunkers facing his men, destroying the first with an incendiary grenade and neutralizing 2 more by rifle fire. He then raced across an open field, still under enemy fire, to rescue a wounded man who was trapped in a trench. Upon reaching the man, he was faced by an armed enemy soldier whom he killed with a pistol. Moving his comrade to safety and returning to his men, he neutralized the final pocket of enemy resistance by fatally wounding 3 North Vietnamese officers with rifle fire. S/Sgt. Hooper then established a final line and reorganized his men, not accepting treatment until this was accomplished and not consenting to evacuation until the following morning. His supreme valor, inspiring leadership and heroic self-sacrifice were directly responsible for the company's success and provided a lasting example in personal courage for every man on the field. S/Sgt. Hooper's actions were in keeping with the highest traditions of the military service and reflect great credit upon himself and the U.S. Army.

Kenneth Michael Kays

Rank and organization: Private First Class, U.S. Army, Headquarters and Headquarters Company, 1st Battalion, 506th Infantry, 101st Airborne Division.
Place and date: Thua Thien province, Republic of Vietnam, 7 May 1970.
Entered service at: Fairfield, Ill.
Born: 22 September 1949, Mount Vernon, Ill.
Citation: For conspicuous gallantry intrepidity in action at the risk of his life above and beyond the call of duty. Pfc. (then Pvt.) Kays distinguished himself while serving as a medical aidman with Company D, 1st Battalion, 101st Airborne Division near Fire Support Base Maureen. A heavily armed force of enemy sappers and infantrymen assaulted Company D's night defensive position, wounding and killing a number of its members. Disregarding the intense enemy fire and ground assault, Pfc. Kays began moving toward the perimeter to assist his fallen comrades. In doing so he became the target of concentrated enemy fire and explosive charges, 1 of which severed the lower portion of his left leg. After applying a tourniquet to his leg, Pfc. Kays moved to the fire-swept perimeter, administered medical aid to 1 of the wounded, and helped move him to an area of relative safety. Despite his severe wound and excruciating pain, Pfc. Kays returned to the perimeter in search of other wounded men. He treated another wounded comrade, and, using his own body as a shield against enemy bullets and fragments, moved him to safety. Although weakened from a great loss of blood, Pfc. Kays resumed his heroic lifesaving efforts by moving beyond the company's perimeter into enemy held territory to treat a wounded American lying there. Only after his fellow wounded soldiers had been treated and evacuated did Pfc. Kays allow his own wounds to be treated. These courageous acts by Pfc. Kays resulted in the saving of numerous lives and inspired others in his company to repel the enemy. Private Kays' heroism at the risk of his life is in keeping with the highest traditions of the service and reflect great credit on him, his unit, and the U.S. Army.

Joseph G. LaPointe Jr.

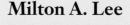

Rank and organization: Specialist Fourth Class, U.S. Army, 2d Squadron, 17th Cavalry, 101st Airborne Division.

Place and date: Quang Tin province, Republic of Vietnam, 2 June 1969.

Entered service at: Cincinnati, Ohio.

Born: 2 July 1948, Dayton, Ohio.

Citation: For conspicuous gallantry and intrepidity in action at the risk of his life above and beyond the call of duty. Sp4c. LaPointe, Headquarters and Headquarters Troop, 2d Squadron, distinguished himself while serving as a medical aidman during a combat helicopter assault mission. Sp4c. LaPointe's patrol was advancing from the landing zone through an adjoining valley when it suddenly encountered heavy automatic weapons fire from a large enemy force entrenched in well fortified bunker positions. In the initial hail of fire, 2 soldiers in the formation vanguard were seriously wounded. Hearing a call for aid from 1 of the wounded, Sp4c. LaPointe ran forward through heavy fire to assist his fallen comrades. To reach the wounded men, he was forced to crawl directly in view of an enemy bunker. As members of his unit attempted to provide covering fire, he administered first aid to 1 man, shielding the other with his body. He was hit by a burst of fire from the bunker while attending the wounded soldier. In spite of his painful wounds, Sp4c. LaPointe continued his lifesaving duties until he was again wounded and knocked to the ground. Making strenuous efforts, he moved back again into a shielding position to continue administering first aid. An exploding enemy grenade mortally wounded all 3 men. Sp4c. LaPointe's courageous actions at the cost of his life were an inspiration to his comrades. His gallantry and selflessness are in the highest traditions of the military service and reflect great credit on him, his unit, and the U.S. Army.

Milton A. Lee

Rank and organization: Private First Class, U.S. Army, Company B, 2d Battalion, 502d Infantry, 1st Brigade, 101st Airborne Division (Airmobile).

Place and date: Near Phu Bai, Thua Thien province, Republic of Vietnam, 26 April 1968.

Entered service at: San Antonio, Tex.

Born: 28 February 1949, Shreveport, La.

Citation: For conspicuous gallantry and intrepidity in action at the risk of his life above and beyond the call of duty. Pfc. Lee distinguished himself near the city of Phu Bai in the province of Thua Thien. Pfc. Lee was serving as the radio telephone operator with the 3d platoon, Company B. As lead element for the company, the 3d platoon received intense surprise hostile fire from a force of North Vietnamese Army regulars in well-concealed bunkers. With 50 percent casualties, the platoon maneuvered to a position of cover to treat their wounded and reorganize, while Pfc. Lee moved through the heavy enemy fire giving lifesaving first aid to his wounded comrades. During the subsequent assault on the enemy defensive positions, Pfc. Lee continuously kept close radio contact with the company commander, relaying precise and understandable orders to his platoon leader. While advancing with the front rank toward the objective, Pfc. Lee observed 4 North Vietnamese soldiers with automatic weapons and a rocket launcher lying in wait for the lead element of the platoon. As the element moved forward, unaware of the concealed danger, Pfc. Lee immediately and with utter disregard for his own personal safety, passed his radio to another soldier and charged through the murderous fire. Without hesitation he continued his assault, overrunning the enemy position, killing all occupants and capturing 4 automatic weapons and a rocket launcher. Pfc. Lee continued his 1-man assault on the second position through a heavy barrage of enemy automatic weapons fire. Grievously wounded, he continued to press the attack, crawling forward into a firing position and delivering accurate covering fire to enable his platoon to maneuver and destroy the position. Not until the position was overrun did Pfc. Lee falter in his steady volume of fire and succumb to his wounds. Pfc. Lee's heroic actions saved the lives of the lead element and were instrumental in the destruction of the key position of the enemy defense. Pfc. Lee's gallantry at the risk of life above and beyond the call of duty are in keeping with the highest traditions of the military service and reflect great credit on himself, the 502d Infantry, and the U.S. Army.

Andre C. Lucas

Rank and organization: Lieutenant Colonel, U.S. Army, 2d Battalion, 506th Infantry, 101st Airborne Division.
Place and date: Fire Support Base Ripcord, Republic of Vietnam, 1 to 23 July 1970. Entered service at: West Point, N.Y.
Born: 2 October 1930, Washington D.C.
Citation: Lt. Col. Lucas distinguished himself by extraordinary heroism while serving as the commanding officer of the 2d Battalion. Although the fire base was constantly subjected to heavy attacks by a numerically superior enemy force throughout this period, Lt. Col. Lucas, forsaking his own safety, performed numerous acts of extraordinary valor in directing the defense of the allied position. On 1 occasion, he flew in a helicopter at treetop level above an entrenched enemy directing the fire of 1 of his companies for over 3 hours. Even though his helicopter was heavily damaged by enemy fire, he remained in an exposed position until the company expended its supply of grenades. He then transferred to another helicopter, dropped critically needed grenades to the troops, and resumed his perilous mission of directing fire on the enemy. These courageous actions by Lt. Col. Lucas prevented the company from being encircled and destroyed by a larger enemy force. On another occasion, Lt. Col. Lucas attempted to rescue a crewman trapped in a burning helicopter. As the flames in the aircraft spread, and enemy fire became intense, Lt. Col. Lucas ordered all members of the rescue party to safety. Then, at great personal risk, he continued the rescue effort amid concentrated enemy mortar fire, intense heat, and exploding ammunition until the aircraft was completely engulfed in flames. Lt. Col. Lucas was mortally wounded while directing the successful withdrawal of his battalion from the fire base. His actions throughout this extended period inspired his men to heroic efforts and were instrumental in saving the lives of many of his fellow soldiers while inflicting heavy casualties on the enemy. Lt. Col. Lucas' conspicuous gallantry and intrepidity in action, at the cost of his own life, were in keeping with the highest traditions of the military service and reflect great credit on him, his unit, and the U.S. Army.

Robert Martin Patterson

Rank and organization: Sergeant, U.S. Army, Troop B, 2d Squadron. 17th Cavalry.
Place and date: Near La Chu, Republic of Vietnam, 6 May 1968.
Entered service at: Raleigh, N.C. Born: 16 April 1948, Durham, N.C.
Citation: For conspicuous gallantry and intrepidity in action at the risk of his life above and beyond the call of duty. Sgt. Patterson (then Sp4c.) distinguished himself while serving as a fire team leader of the 3d Platoon, Troop B, during an assault against a North Vietnamese Army battalion which was entrenched in a heavily fortified position. When the leading squad of the 3d Platoon was pinned down by heavy interlocking automatic weapon and rocket propelled grenade fire from 2 enemy bunkers, Sgt. Patterson and the 2 other members of his assault team moved forward under a hail of enemy fire to destroy the bunkers with grenade and machine-gun fire. Observing that his comrades were being fired on from a third enemy bunker covered by enemy gunners in I-man spider holes, Sgt. Patterson, with complete disregard for his safety and ignoring the warning of his comrades that he was moving

into a bunker complex, assaulted and destroyed the position. Although exposed to intensive small arms and grenade fire from the bunkers and their mutually supporting emplacements, Sgt. Patterson continued his assault upon the bunkers which were impeding the advance of his unit. Sgt. Patterson single-handedly destroyed by rifle and grenade fire 5 enemy bunkers, killed 8 enemy soldiers and captured 7 weapons. His dauntless courage and heroism inspired his platoon to resume the attack and to penetrate the enemy defensive position. Sgt. Patterson's action at the risk of his life has reflected great credit upon himself, his unit, and the U.S. Army.

Gordon R. Roberts

Rank and organization: Sergeant (then Sp4c.), U.S. Army, Company B, 1st Battalion, 506th Infantry, 101st Airborne Division.
Place and date: Thua Thien Province, Republic of Vietnam, 11 July 1969.
Entered service at: Cincinnati, Ohio.
Born: 14 June 1950, Middletown, Ohio.
Citation: For conspicuous gallantry and intrepidity in action at the risk of his life above and beyond the call of duty. Sgt. Roberts distinguished himself while serving as a rifleman in Company B, during combat operations. Sgt. Roberts' platoon was maneuvering along a ridge to attack heavily fortified enemy bunker positions which had pinned down an adjoining friendly company. As the platoon approached the enemy positions, it was suddenly pinned down by heavy automatic weapons and grenade fire from camouflaged enemy fortifications atop the overlooking hill. Seeing his platoon immobilized and in danger of failing in its mission, Sgt. Roberts crawled rapidly toward the closest enemy bunker. With complete disregard for his safety, he leaped to his feet and charged the bunker, firing as he ran. Despite the intense enemy fire directed at him, Sgt. Roberts silenced the 2-man bunker. Without hesitation, Sgt. Roberts continued his I-man assault on a second bunker. As he neared the second bunker, a burst of enemy fire knocked his rifle from his hands. Sgt. Roberts picked up a rifle dropped by a comrade and continued his assault, silencing the bunker. He continued his charge against a third bunker and destroyed it with well-thrown hand grenades. Although Sgt. Roberts was now cut off from his platoon, he continued his assault against a fourth enemy emplacement. He fought through a heavy hail of fire to join elements of the adjoining company which had been pinned down by the enemy fire. Although continually exposed to hostile fire, he assisted in moving wounded personnel from exposed positions on the hilltop to an evacuation area before returning to his unit. By his gallant and selfless actions, Sgt. Roberts contributed directly to saving the lives of his comrades and served as an inspiration to his fellow soldiers in the defeat of the enemy force. Sgt. Roberts' extraordinary heroism in action at the risk of his life were in keeping with the highest traditions of the military service and reflect great credit upon himself, his unit, and the U.S. Army.

Clifford Chester Sims

Rank and organization: Staff Sergeant, U.S. Army, Company D, 2d Battalion (Airborne), 501st Infantry, 101st Airborne Division.
Place and date: Near Hue, Republic of Vietnam, 21 February 1968. Entered service at: Jacksonville, Fla.
Born: 18 June 1942, Port St. Joe, Fla.
Citation: For conspicuous gallantry and intrepidity in action at the risk of his life above and beyond the call of duty. S/Sgt. Sims distinguished himself while serving as a squad leader with Company D. Company D was assaulting a heavily fortified enemy position concealed within a dense wooded area when it encountered strong enemy defensive fire. Once within the woodline, S/Sgt. Sims led his squad in a furious attack against an enemy force which had pinned down the 1st Platoon and threatened to overrun it. His skillful leadership provided the platoon with freedom of movement and enabled it to regain the initiative. S/Sgt. Sims was then ordered to move his squad

to a position where he could provide covering fire for the company command group and to link up with the 3d Platoon, which was under heavy enemy pressure. After moving no more than 30 meters S/Sgt. Sims noticed that a brick structure in which ammunition was stocked was on fire. Realizing the danger, S/Sgt. Sims took immediate action to move his squad from this position. Though in the process of leaving the area 2 members of his squad were injured by the subsequent explosion of the ammunition, S/Sgt. Sims' prompt actions undoubtedly prevented more serious casualties from occurring. While continuing through the dense woods amidst heavy enemy fire, S/Sgt. Sims and his squad were approaching a bunker when they heard the unmistakable noise of a concealed booby trap being triggered immediately to their front. S/Sgt. Sims warned his comrades of the danger and unhesitatingly hurled himself upon the device as it exploded, taking the full impact of the blast. In so protecting his fellow soldiers, he willingly sacrificed his life. S/Sgt. Sims' extraordinary heroism at the cost of his life is in keeping with the highest traditions of the military service and reflects great credit upon himself and the U.S. Army.

Dale Eugene Wayrynen

Rank and organization: Specialist Fourth Class, U.S. Army, Company B, 2d Battalion, 502d Infantry, 1st Brigade, 101st Airborne Division.
Place and date: Quang Ngai, Province, Republic of Vietnam, 18 May 1967.

Entered service at: Minneapolis, Minn.
Born: 18 January 1947, Moose Lake, Minn.
Citation: For conspicuous gallantry and intrepidity in action at the risk of his life above and beyond the call of duty. Sp4c. Wayrynen distinguished himself with Company B, during combat operations near Duc Pho. His platoon was assisting in the night evacuation of the wounded from an earlier enemy contact when the lead man of the unit met face to face with a Viet Cong soldier. The American's shouted warning also alerted the enemy who immediately swept the area with automatic weapons fire from a strongly built bunker close to the trail and threw hand grenades from another nearby fortified position. Almost immediately, the lead man was wounded and knocked from his feet. Sp4c. Wayrynen, the second man in the formation, leaped beyond his fallen comrade to kill another enemy soldier who appeared on the trail, and he dragged his injured companion back to where the point squad had taken cover. Suddenly, a live enemy grenade landed in the center of the tightly grouped men. Sp4c. Wayrynen, quickly assessing the danger to the entire squad as well as to his platoon leader who was nearby, shouted a warning, pushed one soldier out of the way, and threw himself on the grenade at the moment it exploded. He was mortally wounded. His deep and abiding concern for his fellow soldiers was significantly reflected in his supreme and courageous act that preserved the lives of his comrades. Sp4c. Wayrynen's heroic actions are in keeping with the highest traditions of the service, and they reflect great credit upon himself and the U.S. Army.

Chapter 4

AIR ASSETS

After the 101st Airborne returned to its home in Fort Campbell, Kentucky, following the Vietnam War, the unit's tactical air mobility approaches were restructured and refined. On October 4, 1974, the 101st Airborne Division (Air Mobile) became the 101st Airborne Division (Air Assault). The unit no longer requires that all of its personnel obtain airborne qualifications as parachutists, although this is an option. All of its personnel are successful graduates of the prestigious Sabalauski Air Assault School and are thus authorized to wear the Air Assault Badge.

Air assault is more than moving troops and equipment by air. It is a way of executing warfare. As delineated in *Army Field Manual 90-4*, air-assault operations are manned by highly mobile teams covering extensive distances and engaging enemy forces behind enemy lines and often by surprise, as they are usually masked by darkness. The 101st Airborne Division's successful air-assault operations in Vietnam drew on its years of ongoing combat experience. In the 1970s and 1980s, the air-assault division earned a place in the army's new operational doctrine called AirLand Battle, which was successfully demonstrated in the war against Iraq.

AirLand Battle is based on the belief that initiative, depth, agility, and synchronization successfully complete a mission. First, all soldiers are encouraged to take the initiative to seize and exploit opportunities to gain advantages over the enemy. Second, commanders are urged to utilize the entire depth of the battlefield and strike at rear targets that support frontline enemy troops. Third, agility requires commanders to strike the enemy quickly where most vulnerable and to respond to the enemy's strengths. Fourth, synchronization calls for the commander to maximize available combined arms firepower for critical targets to achieve the greatest effect.

Air-assault operations are well matched for AirLand Battle, and the 101st Airborne Division is a commensurate fit. The division contains nine infantry battalions organized into three brigades. Each infantry battalion is authorized approximately forty officers and 640 enlisted personnel; a battalion is organized into a headquarters company, three rifle companies, and an antiarmor company to provide extra firepower against enemy tanks. An aviation brigade with eight battalions provides the 101st Airborne Division with reconnaissance, attack, aeromedical, assault, and logistical lift capabilities. Divisional combat support and combat service support elements complete the unit's organization, and additional units can be attached to the division as necessary.

Assisting the 101st Airborne Division is an extensive array of technologically advanced support elements, equipment, and training resources. Two instrumental assets are the warrant officer and aviation officer.

Right: Specialist Emilio Rodriguez from the 1st Squadron, 33rd Cavalry Regiment, 3rd Brigade Combat Team, 101st Airborne Division, stands guard atop Mount Sin Jar overlooking the Syrian border. *U.S. Army photo by Staff Sergeant Russell Lee Klika*

Opposite: Iraqi Army and U.S. Army soldiers secure a landing zone after departing from a UH-60 Blackhawk helicopter during an assault mission in Iraq, near the Syrian border, on March 6, 2006. *DOD photo by Staff Sergeant Aaron Allmon, U.S. Air Force*

No Mercy

On October 22, 2005, Lieutenant Colonel Doug Gabram, commander of the 1st Battalion, 101st Aviation Regiment, runs a preflight check of the AH-64D Longbow Apache prior to another mission from FOB Speicher, Iraq (below right). The 1st Battalion, 101st Aviation Regiment—the "expect no mercy" Battalion—is the premier attack-helicopter battalion in the U.S. Army and has a lethal fleet of twenty-four AH-64D Longbow Apaches. The 1-101st first gained notoriety during Operation Desert Storm in 1991, when it fired the first shots of the Gulf War during Operation Normandy, destroying key Iraqi radar sites and creating a safe corridor for U.S. aircraft to commence the air campaign. The battalion again proved itself during Operation Iraqi Freedom in 2003 and 2004, conducting several mobile strike-deep attacks during major combat operations, followed by eight months of quick reaction force,

reconnaissance, and VIP security missions during stability and support operations. After a rigorous nineteen months of training and maintenance back at Fort Campbell, Kentucky, the battalion deployed to Iraq for its second tour. Since returning to Iraq, it has conducted an aggressive relief in place/transfer of authority (REP/TOA) with the 8-229th Aviation Regiment from Fort Knox, Kentucky. The battalion was on track to fly more than a thousand combat hours in October 2005. Initial combat missions involved teams of two battalion aircraft along with one 8-229th aircraft conducting local-area orientations, which familiarize aircrews with the environment, geography, and units on the ground.

To become an army helicopter pilot, aviation candidates first complete physical, mental, and emotional evaluation processes. A psychologist interviews each applicant. Physical testing includes the Army Physical Fitness Test. Candidates also must appear before a board of officers and experts who evaluate their performance and potential. These soldiers must be mentally, physically, and emotionally prepared to participate in combat missions.

Candidates undergo weeks of classroom training in basic flight skills, which covers the helicopter aircraft inside and out, flight physics, flight systems, communication systems, and intensive navigation training. Then the aircraft becomes the pilot's classroom. Basic combat flight skills are covered in weeks of training in army helicopters such as the OH-58 Kiowa, UH-60 Blackhawk, CH-47 Chinook, and AH-64 Apache. The aviators learn the tactics for inserting

A CH-47 Chinook helicopter belonging to the 101st Airborne Division takes off from Camp New Jersey in Kuwait, carrying communications equipment for the division's assault command post. *U.S. Army photo by Private First Class James Matise*

Sergeant First Class Arthur "Pete" Chambers of Tigerforce Scout Platoon, 1-327th Infantry Regiment, 101st Airborne Division (Air Assault), pulls security at a tactical control point during Operation Gaugamela in the city of Hawijah, Iraq, on July 20–21, 2006. *Photographer: Specialist Linsay Burnett, 1st Brigade Combat Team, 101st Airborne Division [AA] Public Affairs*

and extracting personnel and equipment loads, possibly behind enemy lines or within hostile areas, and how to accurately employ attack-helicopter capabilities.

Various helicopters and additional aircraft give the 101st Airborne Division exceptional aerial mobility, serve as weapons platforms, and transport soldiers and supplies.

Little Birds

The AH-6 and MH-6 Little Bird helicopters are direct descendents of the Hughes OH-6A Cayuse light-observation helicopters used during the Vietnam War. The AH-6 is an attack version used in close aerial support for ground troops and direct action. The MH-6 is a utility aircraft used to insert or extract small combat teams. Little Birds are capable of hot-weather, high-altitude flight. They boast the lowest maintenance-to-flight-hour ratio in the special operations

aviation fleet. Equipped with forward-looking infrared (FLIR) sensors, these agile and silent helicopters have an increased environmental advantage, operational effectiveness, and the ability to survive the battlefield. The AH-6 can cruise at speeds of 260 kilometers per hour, while the MH-6 has a maximum speed of 280 kilometers per hour. The helicopters' pilots have a choice of five secure radio networks, which includes one satellite communications network (SATCOM) for communicating with other helicopters, ground troops, or commanders aboard naval vessels.

The Mission Enhanced Little Bird (MELB) program updated the AH-6/MH-6 helicopter fleet with a six-bladed main rotor, canted four-bladed tail rotor, 600 shaft horsepower (shp) main transmission drive system, and improved engine inlet. Mission Enhanced Little Bird AH-6 helicopters can be configured to carry an extensive armament depending on the

Major Units of the 101st Airborne Division (Air Assault)

The 101st Airborne Division (Air Assault) is formed from four brigade combat teams plus Division Artillery, Division Support Command, 101st Aviation Brigade, 159th Aviation Brigade, 101st Corps Support Group, and several separate commands. These units have a proud history with the 101st Airborne Division (Air Assault), and as a result, many have adopted nicknames.

1st Brigade Combat Team—*Bastonge*

Headquarters/Headquarters Company, 1st Brigade Combat Team—*Warriors*

1st Battalion, 327th Infantry Regiment—*Above the Rest*

2nd Battalion, 327th Infantry Regiment—*No Slack*

3rd Battalion, 327th Reconnaissance, Surveillance, and Targe Acquisition—*Battleforce*

2nd Battalion, 320th Field Artillery Regiment—*Balls of the Eagle*

326th Brigade Troops Battalion

426th Brigade Support Battalion—*Taskmasters*

2nd Brigade Combat Team—*Strike*

Headquarters/Headquarters Company, 2nd Brigade

1st Battalion, 502nd Infantry Regiment—*First Strike!*

2nd Battalion, 502nd Infantry Regiment—*Strike Force*

3rd Battalion, 502nd Reconnaissance, Surveillance, and Target Acquisition—*Widowmakers*

311th Brigade Troops Battalion—*Team*

526th Brigade Support Battalion—*Best by Performance*

1st Battalion, 320th Field Artillery Regiment—*Top Guns*

3rd Brigade Combat Team—*Rakkasans*

Headquarters/Headquarters Company, 3rd Brigade

1st Battalion, 187th Infantry Regiment—*Leader Rakkasans*

2nd Battalion, 187th Infantry Regiment—*Raider Rakkasans*

3rd Battalion, 187th Reconnaissance Squadron—*Iron Rakkasans*

3rd Battalion, 320th Field Artillery Regiment—*Red Knights*

626th Brigade Support Battalion—*Assurgam*

3rd Battalion, 81st Brigade Troops Battalion

4th Brigade Combat Team—*Currahee*

Headquarters/Headquarters Company, 4th Brigade

1st Battalion, 4th Brigade Combat Team—*Red Curahee*

2nd Battalion, 4th Brigade Combat Team—*Renegades*

3rd Battalion, 4th Reconnaissance, Surveillance, and Target Acquisition

4th Battalion, 320th Field Artillery Regiment—*Tomahawk*

801st Brigade Support Battalion

4th Brigade Troops Battalion—*Strength in Versatility*

101st Aviation Brigade—*Wings of Destiny*

Headquarters/Headquarters Company, Aviation Brigade—*Hellcats*

2nd Battalion, 17th Calvary Regiment—*Out Front!*

1st Battalion, 101st Aviation Regiment—*Expect No Mercy*

2nd Battalion, 101st Aviation Regiment—*Eagle Warrior*

5th Battalion, 101st Aviation Regiment—*Eagle Assault*

6th Battalion, 101st Aviation Regiment—*Shadow of the Eagle*

8th Battalion, 101st Aviation Regiment—*Wings of the Eagle*

159th Aviation Brigade—*Eagle Thunder*

3rd Battalion, 101st Aviation Regiment—*Eagle Attack*

4th Battalion, 101st Aviation Regiment—*Wings of the Eagle*

7th Battalion, 101st Aviation Regiment General Support—*Eagle Lift!*

9th Battalion, 101st Aviation Regiment—*Eagle Strike!*

1st Battalion, 17th Cavalry Regiment—*Pale Horse*

Separate Division Units

2nd Battalion, 44th Air Defense Artillery Battalion—*Strike Fear!*

86th Combat Support Hospital

887th Engineer Company—*Empire*

101st Sustainment Brigade—*Life Liners*

Division Material Management Center

63rd Chemical Company

106th Transportation Battalion

372nd Transportation Company

594th Maintenance Transportation Company

613th Movement Control Team

632nd Movement Control Team

129th Combat Support Battalion

494th Transportation Company

561st Combat Support Battalion

95th Maintenance

102nd Quartermaster Company

196th Quartermaster Detachment

227th Group Support Supply Company

541st Transportation Company

584th Maintenance Company

717th Explosive Ordnance Disposal Detachment

101st Sustainment Brigade Troops Battalion

101st Soldier Support Battalion

specific mission and the helicopter's variant. Updated mission equipment includes lightweight planks, strap-on/off technology, a lightweight Hellfire missile system, and an integrated weapon management system. The lightweight planks provide not only a universal mounting platform for weapons, but also mounting for external conformal fuel tanks and an external capacity for personnel.

The AH-6 has a crew of two and holds no passengers within its fuselage, but it boasts an armament of seven-shot or twelve-shot 70mm Hydra rocket launchers, M134 7.62mm miniguns, MK19 40mm grenade launchers, and air-to-air Stinger missiles. The miniguns are capable of firing 1,980 rounds per minute. A 30mm chain gun can be fired at rates of up to 750 rounds per minute. It can be configured with other armament options such as 2.75-inch rockets, Hellfire laser-guided missiles, a 30mm cannon, and a .50-caliber machine gun.

To provide air support for a unit as mobile as the 101st Airborne Division, the AH-6J Special Attack Aircraft was developed. Based on a small, two-seat civilian helicopter similar to the military's OH-6A Cayuse, the AH-6J version fits aboard a C-130 cargo plane and can be unpacked and ready to fly five minutes after arrival. Its standard armament includes 2.75-inch rocket pods and Gatling-type 7.62mm miniguns.

The MH-6's principal task is transporting special operations forces into tight situations. The troops ride on two planks that are attached to the aircraft's skids, enabling the troops to disembark immediately upon reaching their destination. The MH-6 requires a flight crew of two and accommodates a passenger load of up to six. This light-utility helicopter has a maximum wartime infiltration radius of 518 kilometers. The MH-6 does not routinely accommodate its own armament, but instead relies upon the individual soldier's firepower. In accordance with the MELB programs, artillery can be mounted on its external planks if necessary.

The enhanced and upgraded MH-6 includes structural modifications to increase its maximum take-off weight to 2,367 kilograms. This elevated weight allowance allows for the crew, weapon systems, empty sixty-five-gallon range external auxiliary fuel tanks, toolboxes, personal gear, and mission cargo such as the air assault troops themselves, plus the aircraft's standard fuel capacity of 202 kilograms.

Sergeant Gustavo Gutierrez, a team leader for the Tigerforce Scout Platoon, 1-327th Infantry Regiment, 1st Brigade Combat Team, 101st Airborne Division (Air Assault), scans his sector while pulling security in the city of Hawijah, Iraq, during Operation Gaugamela, on July 20–21, 2006. *Photographer: Specialist Linsay Burnett, 1st Brigade Combat Team, 101st Airborne Division [AA] Public Affairs*

Cobras

The Bell AH-1 Cobra traces its roots to the UH-1 Huey, which was developed and widely used in the mid-1960s during the Vietnam War. Originally, it was designed for close air support (CAS), armed escort for transport helicopters and ground movements, armed and visual reconnaissance, helicopter air-to-air attack, and coordination of artillery and gunfire. Subsequent versions have prevailed in every U.S. military operation since the Vietnam War.

The AH-1 Super Cobra is a twin-engine attack helicopter capable of land- and sea-based operations day or night and in adverse weather conditions, if necessary. In the Cobra, it is the rear-seat pilot who primarily maneuvers the helicopter. The front-seat pilot controls the helicopter's weapons systems, but also has access to a full set of aircraft controls.

Kiowa

The Bell OH-58D Kiowa Warrior is the U.S. Army's armed reconnaissance aircraft. The original OH-58 Kiowa was introduced during the Vietnam War and has evolved into the OH-58D (R). Working as an airborne command post, communications relay station, and reconnaissance observation unit, the Kiowa can instantly convey information about flights, distances, terrain, targets, and enemy positions to attack aircraft in real-time through digital data links connected with the AH-64 Apache and A-10 Thunderbolt aircraft. The Kiowa Warrior is equipped with a mast-mounted

Soldiers from the 1st Squadron, 33rd Cavalry Regiment, 3rd Brigade Combat Team, 101st Airborne Division, prepare to clear a home during a patrol in Salah Ad Din, Iraq, on July 6, 2006, as part of a nine-day operation in search of insurgents. *U.S. Army photo by Staff Sergeant Russell Lee Klika*

Sergeant Michael Fiorella from B Company, 4-320th Field Artillery Battalion, 101st Division, provides security during the Iraqi police academy graduation in the Muthana Zayuna district of Baghdad on January 9, 2005. *U.S. Army photo by Specialist Teddy Wade*

sight, which includes a television system, a thermal imaging system, a laser rangefinder/designator, and an embedded global-positioning system inertial navigation system.

This maneuverable aircraft can land on unimproved airfields. The Kiowa is capable of mounting two weapons systems, including Hellfire missiles, air-to-air Stinger missiles, 2.75-inch Hydra 70 rockets, and/or a 50-caliber fixed machine gun. Through an army reorganization and modernization plan, the OH-58 Kiowa series helicopters, along with the AH-1 Cobras, are slated to be replaced by AH-64D Apache attack helicopters and RAH-66 Comanche reconnaissance helicopters.

Apache

The Boeing McDonnell Douglas AH-64 Apache is the U.S. Army's primary attack helicopter, specifically designed to destroy highly valued targets with the Hellfire missile. Its superior capabilities and technology, which includes the

Staff Sergeant Jacob Sprenger and Private First Class Dewayne White, from A Company, 1-327th Infantry Regiment, 101st Airborne Division, provide security at a vehicle checkpoint on December 4, 2006. Soldiers from A Company were conducting vehicle and personnel searches on a main road outside of Hawijah, Iraq, where days earlier one of their vehicles was hit by a vehicle-borne improvised explosive device. *U.S. Army photo by Specialist Timothy Kingston*

target acquisition designation sight (TADS) and a pilot night vision sensor (PNVS), allow its crew to maneuver over diverse terrain and to attack targets during the day and night and in adverse weather throughout the world. The 17,650-pound helicopter can cruise at airspeeds of 145 miles per hour and boasts a flight endurance of more than three hours, which is easily extended with an additional 230-gallon external fuel tank.

The twin-engine, four-bladed attack helicopter has a highly stable aerial weapons-delivery platform. The Apache can carry up to sixteen Hellfire laser designated missiles, which are used primarily for destroying tanks, armored vehicles, and other hard material targets at a range of up to eight thousand meters. The Apache can also deliver seventy-six 2.75-inch folding fin aerial rockets for use against enemy personnel and light-armor vehicles. Furthermore, the Apache is equipped with 1,200 rounds of ammunition for its area weapons system (AWS), a 30mm automatic gun. The AH-64A can be converted to an AH-64D Longbow by applying technological improvements such as the glass cockpit display, advanced engines, wiring for Longbow systems, a radar interferometer, a Longbow millimeter wave fire-control radar, and the Longbow missile system.

To maneuver these multimillion-dollar aircraft, pilots are fitted for a specifically designed integrated helmet and display sighting system (IHADSS), which serves as a platform for a helmet mounted display (HMD). The HMD provides pilots with flight control imagery and flight information.

Soldiers from A Company, 1-327th Infantry Regiment, 101st Airborne Division, along with Iraqi soldiers, prepare to leave FOB McHenry on a joint patrol outside of Hawijah, Iraq, on December 4, 2006. *U.S. Army photo by Specialist Timothy Kingston*

Blackhawk

The Sikorsky-made MH-60A Blackhawk has evolved into three separate varieties: the MH-60G, which is known as the Pave Hawk and is used by the U.S. Air Force Special Operations Wings, and the MH-60L and MH-60K, both of which are utilized by the 160th SOAR(A). The MH-60 variants of the original Blackhawk are the army's medium-sized utility helicopter. The Blackhawk variants were among the first helicopters to be equipped with FLIR sensors, a "Disco Light" infrared (IR) jammer, a global positioning system (GPS), auxiliary fuel tanks, infrared suppressive exhausts, SATCOM radios, radar warning receivers, 7.62mm miniguns, and other numerous other cutting-edge, special operations technological features. The MH-60 series helicopters can operate from a fixed land facility, remote land site, or ocean vessel.

In the late 1980s, the MH-60L was introduced. The MH-60L was only about halfway through its operational evaluation when Iraq invaded Kuwait in 1990. The upgrade process was accelerated, and several of the L models were able to serve in Operations Desert Shield and Storm alongside the original Blackhawk type-A models. The MH-60L's upgrades give it aerial refueling capability, electronics such as color Doppler weather radar, Kevlar

Left: Specialist Enriquillo Hernandez provides security as his platoon leader gathers intelligence along the Syria/Iraq border near FOB Nimur, Iraq, on August 13, 2006. Hernandez is with 1st Squadron, 33rd Cavalry Regiment, 3rd Brigade Combat Team, 101st Airborne Division. *U.S. Army photo by Staff Sergeant Russell Lee Klika*

Below: A Longbow Apache, from Task Force No Mercy, 1st Battalion, 101st Combat Aviation Brigade, provides air support during an aerial-traffic-control-point mission near Tall Afar, Iraq, on July 2, 2006. *Photo by Staff Sergeant Jacob N. Bailey*

Soldiers from the A Battery, 3rd Battalion, 320th Field Artillery Regiment, 101st Division, stay low to the ground as a CH-47 Chinook comes in to pick them up after a morning raid in support of Operation Red Light in Remagen, Iraq, on February 24, 2006. *U.S. Navy Photo by Photographer's Mate Third Class [AW] Shawn Hussong, Fleet Combat Camera, Atlantic*

ballistic armor, and the ability to carry Hellfire missiles. A new folding tail was added to simplify its use aboard naval vessels. Despite the MH-60 variant or upgrade, Blackhawks served the airborne and air-assault soldiers as a utility helicopter for the transportation of equipment, infiltration or exfiltration of troops, and close-combat air support during hostile operations.

The MH-60K is the high-end special operations helicopter, saturated with advanced avionics. In addition to the many upgrades on the L model, it features a fully integrated, night-vision goggle (NVG) and compatible glass cockpit with custom-designed liquid-crystal displays for easier use with NVGs. The MH-60K flight deck is designed for flying fast and low at night and when weather conditions make visibility nearly nonexistent. It has terrain-following radar and a FLIR sensor that provides complete weather information combined with "map-of-the-earth" information to enhance pinpoint navigation despite adverse conditions. A laser range finder allows the crew to detect, identify, and engage targets at an extended range with laser-guided missiles. Technologically advanced, laser-guided Hellfire rockets are mounted on either side of the craft's body on detachable "wings."

Soldiers from the 3rd Battalion, 187th Infantry Regiment, along with soldiers from the Iraqi Army's 2nd Battalion, 1st Brigade, 4th Division, launch Operation Swarmer, in the Salah Ad Din province of Iraq on March 16, 2006. *U.S. Navy Photo by Journalist First Class Jeremy Wood*

The Blackhawk direct action penetrator (DAP) version is used primarily for armed escorts and fire support for air assault and other special operations forces. Accordingly, this variant is equipped with integrated fire-control systems and a pilot's heads-up display (HUD) that results in highly accurate and effective firepower. The 160th SOAR(A) pilots designed the DAP version so that it could have weapons configurations of two nineteen-round 70mm rocket pods, two 7.62mm miniguns, two forward-firing 30mm chain-guns, Hellfire rockets, and Stinger missiles. An external hydraulic hoist system can lift 600 pounds with up to 200 feet of cable for rescue operations. Mounted on the helicopter's underside is a cargo hook capable of supporting an external load of nine thousand pounds. A land vehicle can be attached to the external cable by a sling then transported by the Blackhawk and dropped at a new location. The fast-rope insertion/extraction system (FRIES) mounted on either side of the aircraft's body can support 1,500 pounds each. The DAP version can carry twelve to fifteen soldiers and their equipment more than 750 miles without refueling.

Soldiers from the 1st Brigade, 1st Armored Division, dismount a UH-60 Blackhawk from the 101st Airborne Division, Task Force No Mercy, Bravo Company, 1st of the 207 Aviation Division during an air assault in the Al Jazeera Desert of Iraq on March 22, 2006. *U.S. Air Force photo by Staff Sergeant Aaron Allmon*

Chinook

The Boeing MH-47 Chinook and its variants are the army's long-distance, heavy-lift cargo helicopters. Their fast-rope rappelling system, aerial refueling capability, and extensive avionics are similar to those of the MH-60K Blackhawk. Its technological aspects give this heavy aircraft the unique ability to perform long-range flights despite harsh weather conditions, limited visibility, or low ceilings. The MH-47E holds 1,000 gallons of fuel in its internal fuel tanks; of all the army's helicopters, it can fly the longest range without refueling. Chinooks routinely fly six-hour missions. It possesses the same glass cockpit as the MH-60K Blackhawk to enhance nighttime navigation.

Pilots can fly the weighty MH-47 Chinook fast and low to the ground. Its aircrews are specifically trained to support air-assault and other special operations forces by providing armed close air support (CAS) and guidance for

Soldiers from 2nd Battalion, 502nd Infantry Regiment, 101st Airborne Division (Air Assault), conducted Operation Willing Eagle on May 8, 2006, in the city of Sadr Yusufiyah, Iraq. The purpose of the operation was to survey how much more work needed to be done to finish a power plant that the Russians started building in 2001 but stopped years later. A security team escorted a survey team at the plant. *U.S. Army photo by Staff Sergeant Kevin L. Moses Sr.*

On December 9, 2005, Sergeant Chris Schroeder, 3rd Platoon, Alpha Troop, 1st Squadron, 33rd Cavalry, 3rd Brigade, 101st Airborne, provided security for Iraqi contractors moving barriers to polling locations in the village of Al-Mazra'a, outside the city of Baji, Iraq. On December 15, the Iraqi citizens voted to elect the first free, permanent parliamentary government. *U.S. Air Force photo by Technical Sergeant Andy Dunaway*

precise target engagement. Weapon systems in three stations increase the aircraft's lethality. The left forward window and right cabin door each have 7.62mm Gatling-type miniguns, and the rear ramp mounts a M60 7.62-millimeter machine gun.

The expansive cabin provides forty-two cubic meters of cargo space and twenty-one square meters of cargo floor area. It can carry two high-mobility multipurpose wheeled vehicles (HMMWVs) or a single HMMWV with 105mm howitzer and gun crew. The interior is designed so that soldiers can drive the vehicles directly off the rear ramp upon

landing. The cargo area can easily hold Zodiac rubber boats for water operations, and the ramp can function as the launching pad. The main cabin can hold from thirty-three to fifty-five fully equipped troops, depending upon the seating arrangements, along with special operations equipment. It can transport twenty-four "litters"—wounded on gurneys—with two medics. It requires a crew of two pilots and can accommodate a combat commander. A crewman operates each of the three weapons stations.

The Chinook has a triple-hook system for large external loads; the hooks are mounted to the Chinook's belly. The

Master Sergeant Roberto Rodriguez from the Personnel Security Detachment, 1st Brigade, 101st Airborne Division, provides security at a vehicle checkpoint in Kirkuk, Iraq, on December 1, 2005. *U.S. Army photo by Specialist Timothy Kingston*

central hook can carry up to twelve thousand kilograms, and the other two hooks can carry seventy-five hundred kilograms each. These hooks can be used together to stabilize one heavy load or to transport three separate loads.

Pave Low

The Sikorsky MH-53J Pave Low is the U.S. Air Force's heavy-lift, long-range special operations helicopter. First deployed in 1981, the MH-53's airframe and avionics have been continuously and extensively upgraded to expand its operational capabilities. The Pave Low helicopter performs deep-penetration missions in heavily defended airspace at night and in adverse weather conditions. Its missions include search-and-rescue coverage, infiltration and exfiltration, and resupply of special operations forces.

When vertical takeoff and landing is required, the Pave Low's upgraded version, the MH-53J Pave Low IIIE, answers the call. Additional external fuel tanks give it a flight range of 630 miles; with aerial refueling, its range is unlimited. It can fly at altitudes of up to sixteen thousand feet and as low as one hundred feet. Low-altitude maneuvers are made possible by technological advances such as terrain-following and

Sergeant Mitchell Levart, 2nd Platoon, Alpha Company, 1st Battalion, 327 Infantry, 101st Airborne, provides security while his platoon conducts a joint foot patrol with the Iraqi Army in the village of Namla, Iraq, on October 31, 2005. *U.S. Air Force photo by Technical Sergeant Andy Dunaway*

terrain-avoidance radar, a FLIR sensor, SATCOM radios, and a global positioning system. A projected "moving map" display enables the crew to follow terrain contours and avoid obstacles. This navigational system allows the Pave Low to fly at night without detection and arrive on target at the precise time. It can travel at speeds of 165 miles per hour at sea level. This forty-two-thousand-pound helicopter is equipped with radar-warning receivers as well as chaff and flare launchers to help defend the aircraft from enemy missiles.

The Pave Low can be armed with up to three 7.62mm miniguns or .50-caliber machine guns for suppressive fire. Extensive armor covers the vital areas of the aircraft to increase crew and passenger serviceability. Its maximum passenger capacity is thirty-eight troops or fourteen litters, and the craft can sling up to twenty thosuand pounds with its external cargo hook.

The Pave Low requires a crew of two pilots, two enlisted light engineers, and two aerial gunners, whose flight training

Staff Sergeant Justin Orr, a squad leader for the Tigerforce Scout Platoon, 1-327th Infantry Regiment, 101st Airborne Division (Air Assault), looks through the scope of a sniper rifle while pulling security during Operation Gaugamela in the city of Hawijah, Iraq, on July 20–21, 2006. *Photographer: Specialist Linsay Burnett, 1st Brigade Combat Team, 101st Airborne Division [AA] Public Affairs*

takes about eight months to complete. Operating this complicated helicopter requires extensive knowledge and carefully coordinated teamwork. In search and rescue missions, two U.S. Air Force pararescue medics will accompany the crew.

C-130 and C-141

The U.S. Air Force Special Operations Command's Lockheed C-130 Hercules primarily performs the tactical portion of an airlift mission. Versions of the C-130 perform a number of operational missions in both peace and war situations, including airlift support, Antarctic ice resupply, aeromedical missions, firefighting duties for the U.S. Forest Service, and natural-disaster relief missions. For airborne, air-assault, and special operations forces, the C-130 is the transport for mass tactical airborne insertion and air dropping

equipment into hostile areas. Using its aft loading ramp and door, the C-130 can accommodate a wide variety of over-sized cargo, including but not limited to Little Bird helicopters, utility helicopters, six-wheeled armored vehicles, and HMMWVs. Palletized cargo such as motorcycles is dropped from the C-130. For water operations, a squad with combat-rubber raiding craft (CRRC) parachutes into the water from a C-130 aircraft. The C-130E/H/J variants can hold 74 litters, 92 combat troops, 64 paratroopers, or the combination of these. The C-130J-30 version can accommodate 97 litters, 128 combat troops, 92 airborne troops, or a combination of any of these.

The C-130 aircraft can air drop loads up to forty-two thousand pounds. It uses the high-floatation landing gear to land and deliver cargo on rough, dirt strips. The Hercules C-130 E and H variations require a crew of five: two

Staff Sergeant Emanuel Walls from 2nd Platoon, Alpha Company, 1st Battalion, 327 Infantry, 101st Airborne, provides security while his platoon checks random vehicles at a traffic-control point outside the village of Namla, Iraq, on October 31, 2005. *U.S. Air Force photo by Technical Sergeant Andy Dunaway*

U.S. soldiers, Iraqi soldiers, and U.S. aircraft are positioned on the airstrip at FOB Remagen, Iraq, in preparation for Operation Swarmer on March 16, 2006. Operation Swarmer was a combined air-assault operation to clear suspected insurgents from the area northeast of Samarra. The soldiers are from the Iraqi Army's 1st Brigade, 4th Division, and the U.S. Army's 3rd Brigade Combat Team and the 101st Combat Aviation Brigade of the 101st Airborne Division. *DOD photo by Sergeant First Class Antony Joseph, U.S. Army*

pilots, a navigator, a flight engineer, and a loadmaster. The C-130J and C-130J-30 versions require two pilots and a loadmaster.

The Lockheed C-141A, built between 1963 and 1967, was Air Mobility Command's first jet aircraft designed to meet military standards as a troop and cargo carrier. The C-141B Starlifter fulfills the vast spectrum of airlift requirements with its ability to airlift combat forces over long distances; deliver those forces and their equipment either by air, land, or air drop; resupply forces; and transport the sick and wounded from the hostile area to medical facilities. Within the cargo compartment, the C-141 can transition from rollers on the floor for palletized cargo to a smooth floor for wheeled vehicles to aft-facing seats or sidewall canvas seats for passengers. This mammoth aircraft is crewed by two pilots, two flight engineers, and one loadmaster, plus one navigator for air drops. It can transport 200 troops, 155 paratroopers, 103 litters, and 14 seats, or 68,725 pounds of cargo.

Soldiers from the 4th Battalion, 320th Field Artillery Regiment, 101st Airborne Division, and Iraqi police search a field during sweeps on a farm in the Zafaraniya district of Baghdad, Iraq, on December 29, 2005. The sweeps were conducted to search out weapons and items used to make improvised explosive devices. *DOD photo by Private First Class William Servinski II, U.S. Army*

What's in a name?

The 1st Brigade Combat Team is deeply connected to the 327th Infantry Regiment, which participated in the World War II campaigns in Normandy, Ardennes-Alsace forest, Rhineland, and central Europe. And the 327th Infantry Regiment is deeply connected with Bastogne, which led to the closing of the war in Europe. Naming the 1st Brigade Combat Team "Bastogne Brigade" maintains the bonds of brotherhood formed in times of combat and preserves the memory of those who paid the ultimate sacrifice in the line of duty.

With the reorganization of the Combat Arms Regimental System in 1984, the 2nd Brigade of the 101st Airborne Division became the parent unit for the 1st, 2nd, and 3rd Battalions of the 502nd Infantry Regiment. It was at this time the 2nd Brigade Combat Team adopted the regimental motto "Strike."

Over the years, the 187th Infantry Regiment has incurred several reorganizations and redesignations, and has finally become the 3rd Brigade Combat Team of the 101st Airborne Division (Air Assault). In February 1943, the 187th Infantry Regiment was activated as a glider infantry regiment assigned to the 11th Airborne Division. In May 1944, the 187th Regiment was deployed to the southwest Pacific region. In the cover of darkness on December 6, 1944, the Japanese 3rd Parachute Regiment attacked the 187th Regiment. The attack was the beginning of continuous fighting for the next months. The 187th Regiment drove back the enemy and seized the Lipa Airfield on Luzon in the Philippine Islands. Heavy casualties were taken. The fighting in the Philippines continued with air-to-water

assaults and fighting through the dense tropical jungles. On August 30, 1945, at 1:00 am, planes carrying the 187th Infantry Regiment flew from Okinawa and Iwo Jima to the Atsugi Airfield located on Japan's main island of Honshu. The 187th Regiment marked the first American troops to enter Japan in two thousand years. By the day's end, more than 4,200 troops and 123 planes had arrived on the airfield, and those landing included General Douglas McArthur, who accepted the Japanese surrender and assumed duties as the military governor of Japan. While the soldiers of the 187th Regiment served as the American occupation force in Japan, the Japanese bestowed upon the paratroopers the nickname *Rakkasan,* which in Japanese loosely means "falling umbrella."

The 4th Brigade Combat Team traces its roots to the 506th Parachute Infantry Regiment, which was initially activated July 20, 194, at Mount Currahee, Camp Toccoa, Georgia. The 506th Parachute Infantry Regiment was part of the newly established 101st Airborne Division. Led by their regimental commander Colonel Robert F. Sink, the 506th Regiment completed a 137-mile road march from Camp Toccoa to Airborne School at Fort Benning, Georgia. These soldiers were the first to complete airborne training as a unit. From their beginnings in the wooded hills of Cherokee Indian territory in northern Georgia, the 506th adopted the Cherokee word *Currahee* meaning "stands alone." Although the 506th Parachute Infantry Regiment was formally deactivated in May 1984, its distinguished legacy stands alone.

Chapter 5

MODERN DAY SCREAMING EAGLES

For approximately fifteen years following the Vietnam War, the 101st Airborne Division (Air Assault) did not experience combat in the arena of warfare, but participated in many combat-related trainings, demonstrations of force, joint task-force exercises, and peace-keeping assignments. Such activities took place in the United States, Germany, Honduras, and Egypt.

In 1976, the 101st Airborne Division returned to European soil for the first time since World War II. The unit participated in Reforger 76, an exercise testing the incorporation of air-assault tactics with West German mechanized units and an American armored cavalry regiment. Its purpose was to maintain a state of preparedness in case of a Soviet attack on West Germany. The exercises were completed and tactics were proven as effective. The 101st Division continued its proven record of professionalism and military prowess at the North Atlantic Treaty Organization's partnership training with units from Belgium, Great Britain, West Germany, and the Netherlands.

In November 1980, elements of the 101st Airborne Division participated in the Rapid Deployment Joint Task Force exercise Bright Star near Cairo, Egypt. A battalion combat team of approximately 900 men from the 1st Battalion, 501st Infantry, was sent to the area along with support units. This exercise gave the men training in desert warfare, overseas deployment and travel, and integration with other branches of the U.S. military and foreign military allies. This training, and subsequent similar rapid-deployment training exercises, proved vital for later combat-mission deployment.

In March 1982, the 101st Airborne Division's 1st Battalion, 502nd Infantry, was sent to the Sinai Peninsula in Egypt to alternate six-month tours of duty with the 82nd Airborne Division. Their purpose was to serve as a peace-keeping force to support the terms established by the 1979 Egypt-Israeli peace treaty. Various battalions of the 101st participated in these tour of duty rotations. Their service in the Sinai Peninsula was part of the multinational force and observers (MFO).On December 12, 1985, the 3rd Battalion of the 502nd Infantry was returning from a peacekeeping MFO tour in the Sinai Peninsula when its aircraft crashed near Gander, Newfoundland, tragically killing 248 soldiers of the 101st Airborne Division.

Above: General Tommy Franks, CENTCOM commander in chief, addresses Sergeant Lucas Goddard, Bravo Company, 3rd Battalion, and Sergeant James Ward, Charlie Company, 1st Battalion, 327th Infantry Regiment, 101st Airborne Division (Air Assault), before giving them Bronze Stars for valor in combat. *Photo by Private First Class Joshua Hutcheson, division journalist*

Opposite: First Sergeant Arthur Abiera, Apache Troop, 1-33 Cavalry, 3rd Brigade Combat Team, 101st Airborne Division, makes a routine presence patrol on the outskirts of Sadr City, Iraq.

Operation Desert Storm

Under the command of Saddam Hussein, the army of Iraq invaded and captured the neighboring country of Kuwait on August 2, 1990. The United States immediately responded by deploying many units and assets to avoid a possible international crisis. The military transport and build up of force in Saudi Arabia during Operation Desert Shield demonstrated the United States' commitment to defend its ally.

As the 24th Infantry Division (Mechanized) began to mobilize, the 101st Airborne Division's advance party was sent to lay the ground work for the remaining Screaming Eagles and other units from the 229th Aviation, which was equipped with Apache attack helicopters, and 9th Cavalry,

Specialist Robert D. Casturao (foreground) and Staff Sergeant Matthew Carothers, both with the 1st Squadron, 61st Cavalry Regiment, 506th Regimental Combat Team, 101st Airborne Division, provide overwatch security during an engagement with insurgents in the Shaab neighborhood of northeast Baghdad on October 2, 2006. Soldiers responded to shots fired at patrolling Iraqi national police officers and remained on the scene until a platoon of Iraqi soldiers arrived to relieve them. *U.S. Navy photo by Petty Officer First Class Keith W. DeVinney*

which was equipped with reconnaissance Kiowa helicopters. The first units from the 101st Airborne Division were deployed to Saudi Arabia on August 17, 1990. The initial force of 2,742 troops, 117 helicopters, 487 combat vehicles, and 123 pallets of supplies was transported on more than a hundred U.S. Air Force C-5 and C-141 aircraft. The remainder of the 101st Airborne Division (Air Assault) was transported by road and rail to Jacksonville, Florida, for deployment to Saudi Arabia aboard U.S. Navy transport ships. The first of ten ships transporting the 101st Division's equipment left the Florida port on August 19, 1990, and the last debarked on September 10, 1990. After a month's time, the ships arrived in the Persian Gulf and at the Saudi port of

Ad Daman. All of the 101st Airborne Division's elements and assets were in Saudi Arabia by October 6, 1990. The 101st Airborne, under the command of Major General J. H. Binford Peay III, was the first U.S. Army division to have all of its assets in the theater and poised for its mission.

Shortly after the massive American force arrived on Saudi soil, the 101st Division moved to King Faud International Airport and established a secure base, Camp Eagle II, surrounded by miles upon miles of concertina wire and sandbags. All of the troops, regardless of their formal MOS, helped secure the base camp. Rifles were issued to everyone, regardless of their occupation specialty. Even the 101st Division band doubled as security for the division's tactical

84

Soldiers with the 1st Squadron, 61st Cavalry Regiment, 506th Regimental Combat Team, 101st Airborne Division, position their vehicles in a standard diamond pattern, which creates a safe defensive position, in order to engage insurgents in the Shaab neighborhood of northeast Baghdad on October 2, 2006. The soldiers responded to shots fired at patrolling Iraqi national police officers and remained on the scene until a platoon of Iraqi Army soldiers arrived to relieve them. *U.S. Navy photo by Petty Officer First Class Keith W. DeVinney*

On April 7, 2003, General Tommy Franks, CENTCOM commander in chief, studies a weapons cache discovered by the 1st Brigade, 101st Airborne Division, (Air Assault), at an Iraqi military training compound in the city of Najaf. Behind him, Major General David H. Petraeus, division commander, looks on. *Photo by Private First Class Joshua Hutcheson, division journalist*

operations center. About 130 miles northwest of Camp Eagle II and 85 miles south of the Kuwait border, the division established a defensive area of operations (AO) named Normandy, which encompassed an 1,800-square-mile region. Within their AO Normandy, the 101st Division was at the ready at Forward Operating Base (FOB) Bastogne, located near An Nu'ayriyah, and FOB Oasis, located in AO Normandy's western sector.

The assault on occupied Kuwait would encompass the forces of not only the 101st Airborne Division and units attached to the division, but also the 82nd Airborne Division, the French 6th Light Armored Division, and other international forces and material as well. Their mission: liberate Kuwait.

At 2:38 a.m. on January 17, 1991, eight AH-64 Apache helicopters of the 101st fired the first shots of Operation Desert Storm. They destroyed two of the Iraqi early warning radar sites, which cleared the avenue of approach for U.S. Air Force aircraft on their way to Baghdad. Apache gunships continued to attack Iraqi air-defense positions. Blackhawk helicopters hovered close to the scene in case aircraft were shot down and pilots needed rescue. Hundreds of sorties attacked the various strategic Iraqi positions over the next month. In mid-February, aviation units stepped aside for the ground war.

On the dawn of February 24, 1991, three hundred helicopters airlifted the 101st Airborne Division troops, launching the largest helicopter air assault in the history of modern warfare. More than two thousand men, fifty transport vehicles, artillery, ammunition, and tons of fuel were airlifted into Iraq. Despite their numbers, they achieved a surprise infiltration deep inside the Iraqi border and descended upon their objective, FOB Cobra. Most of the Iraqi forces there were taken as prisoners. The 101st continued another fifty to sixty miles into Iraq. By nightfall, the division cut off Highway 8, a vital supply line running between Basra and the Iraqi forces in Baghdad.

On the morning of February 25, 1991, the 3rd Brigade of the 187th Infantry Regiment, nicknamed the "Rakkasans," moved north to its objective on the southern bank of the Euphrates River, a region named AO Eagle. It conducted the largest and deepest air-assault operation in history, as it struck 155 miles behind enemy lines into the Euphrates River Valley. This element of the 101st Airborne Division

Commanders of the 101st Airborne Division (Air Assault)

Major General William C. Lee: August 1942–February 1944

Major General Maxwell D. Taylor: March 1944–December 1944

Brigadier General William Gillmore: August 1945–September 1945

Brigadier General Gerald St. Clair Mickle: September 1945–October 1945

Brigadier General Stuart Cutler: October 1945–November 1945

(Division inactive: 30 November 1945–6 July 1948)

Major General William R. Schmidt: July 1948–May 1949

(Division inactive: 27 May 49–25 Aug 50)

Major General Cornelius E. Ryan: August 1950–May 1951

Major General Roy E. Porter: June 1951–May 1953

Major General Paul DeWitt Adams: May 1953–December 1953

(Division inactive: 1 December 1953–15 May 1954)

Major General Riley F. Ennis: May 1954–October 1955

Major General F. S. Bowen: October 1955–March 1956

(Division inactivated on March 1956, moved to Fort Campbell, Kentucky)

Major General Thomas L. Sherbourne Jr.: May 1956–March 1958

Major General William C. Westmoreland: April 1958–June 1960

Major General Ben Harrell: June 1960–July 1961

Major General Charles W. G. Rich: July 1961–February 1963

Major General Harry W. Critz: February 1963–March 1964

Major General Beverly E. Powell: March 1964–March 1966

Major General Ben Sternberg: March 1966–July 1967

Major General Olinto M. Barsanti: July 1967–July 1968

Major General Melvin Zais: July 1968–May 1969

Major General John Wright: May 1969–May 1970

Major General John J. Hennessey: May 1970–February 1971

Major General Thomas M. Tarpley: February 1971–April 1972

Major General John W. Cushman: April 1972–August 1973

Major General Sidney B. Berry: August 1973–July 1974

Major General John W. McEnery: August 1974–February 1976

Major General John A. Wickham Jr.: March 1976–March 1978

Major General John N. Brandenburg: March 1978–June 1980

Major General Jack V. Mackmull: June 1980–August 1981

Major General Charles W. Bagnal: August 1981–August 1983

Major General James E. Thompson: August 1983–June 1985

Major General Burton D. Patrick: June 1985–May 1987

Major General Teddy G. Allen: May 1987–August 1989

Major General J. H. Binford Peay III: August 1989–June 1991

Major General John E. Miller: June 1991–July 1993

Major General John M. Keane: July 1993–February 1996

Major General William F. "Buck" Kernan: February 1996–February1998

Major General Robert T. Clark: February1998–June 2000

Major General Richard A. Cody: June 2000–July 2002

Major General David H. Petraeus : July 2002–May 2004

Major General Thomas R. Turner : May 2004–present

Major General Jeffrey J. Schloesser: Announced

Note: Brigadier General Don F. Pratt (6 February 1944–14 March 1944) and Brigadier General Anthony C. McAuliffe (5 December 1944–26 December 1944) were not included on this list because they were acting division commanders during these times.

met little Iraqi resistance and took its objective with relative efficiency. This action led to the timely defeat of Iraqi forces and helped ensure a total allied victory. The 101st Airborne Division maintained their positions at FOB Cobra, Highway 8, and the Euphrates River while waiting for coalition forces to attack. The position of AO Eagle placed the 101st Airborne Division's forces a mere 145 miles southeast of Baghdad.

Over the next two days, men of the 101st Airborne Division began accepting the surrender of thousands of Iraqi

A sergeant from the Tigerforce Scout Platoon, 1-327th Infantry Regiment, 1st Brigade Combat Team, 101st Airborne Division (Air Assault), stands guard during a cordon and search in a village in the Hawijah district, on July 17–18, 2006. *Photographer: Specialist Linsay Burnett, 1st Brigade Combat Team, 101st Airborne Division [AA] Public Affairs*

troops in retreat from the massive ground assault. FOB Viper was established to address the Iraqi troops withdrawing from the Kuwait border. In one hundred hours of combat, the 101st Airborne Division completed the most efficient and effective combat-helicopter assault ever attempted. After a ceasefire was established on February 27, 1991, the division prepared for redeployment; the unit was deployed home to Fort Campbell in April and remained there through May 1991. The 101st Airborne Division did not incur combat deaths during the ground war. The 2nd Battalion, 229th Aviation, attached to the 101st Airborne Division tragically lost five soldiers while conducting a search-and-rescue mission

for an air-force pilot. Their Blackhawk helicopter was shot down by enemy fire. Five crew members were killed and three others were captured; they were later released.

The Global War on Terrorism

The 101st Airborne Division was called to Afghanistan to relieve the 26th Marine Expeditionary Unit in support of operations aiming to destroy the Al Qaeda terrorist network and Taliban regimen. The unit arrived in January 2002 and would remain in the mountains of Afghanistan until mid-2002. On March 2, 2002, elements of the 101st Airborne Division were sent to conduct an air-assault raid on a terrorist

Sergeant Jose Rivera and his team, Bravo Company, 1st Battalion, 187 Infantry Regiment, 3rd Brigade Combat Team, 101st Airborne, wait for the signal to enter a house while conducting a foot patrol in the city of Bayji, Iraq, on December 10, 2005. *U.S. Air Force photo by Technical Sergeant Andy Dunaway*

During a main supply road patrol in Tikrit, Iraq, on April 23, 2006, Staff Sergeant Brad Smith from the 3-320th Field Artillery, 101st Airborne Division, shot a suspicious object sitting in the middle of the road. *U.S. Army photo by Specialist Teddy Wade*

Parachute Demonstration Team

The 101st Airborne Division (Air Assault) Command Parachute Demonstration Team is an aerial demonstration unit in the U.S. Army. Initially, the team consisted of volunteers who dedicated their personal time to the practice and performance of parachute demonstrations. After its success, the 101st Airborne Division's command group formed a full-time team in 1984. These parachutists proudly represent the 101st Airborne Division's on-going aerial traditions.

The Parachute Demonstration Team's mission is to perform live demonstrations that support U.S. Army's community relationships and promote the army through the sport of skydiving. Demonstrations occur at air shows, professional sporting games, and civic events. The team averages seventy events each year and has conducted more than one thousand demonstrations since their inception. In September 1999, the Parachute Demonstration Team conducted its first international show in Eindhoven, Holland. Although a momentous occasion all on its own, the demonstration had additional significance as well. In was on September 18, 1944, that the 506th Parachute Infantry Regiment, 101st Airborne Division, liberated the town of Eindhoven during Operation Market Garden.

It is an honor and a privilege to be a member of the Parachute Demonstration Team. Members usually work with the team for two years before continuing their careers in their military occupation specialty. The team trains year-round because performing these demonstrations requires specific skill, precise control, and teamwork. Each parachutist holds a professional exhibition rating through the U.S. Parachute Association. The jumpers are trained in all aspects of parachute demonstration ranging from freefall jumps to canopy relative work. To hone their skills, the parachutists make between four hundred and five hundred training jumps each year. In addition to the actual parachute demonstrations, the team covers duties such as show coordination, aviation coordination, media relations, and rigging.

Jumpers fall through the air at speeds of up to 120 miles per hour and exit the aircraft from 2,500 to 10,500 feet above ground level depending upon the type of demonstration they are exhibiting. Demonstrations include two freefall parachutists showing basic flight control by maneuvering their bodies and linking up during freefall. Three of more parachutists exit the aircraft simultaneously and join together to create a large formation in the sky. The team conducts further maneuvers during freefall. They use their bodies to create the illusion of a barber pole spiraling in the sky while freefalling to the ground. Colorful smoke and flags may be incorporated. Instead of deploying their parachute at a lower altitude, jumpers open their parachutes upon exiting the aircraft. On these jumps, the parachutists fly their canopies together and create a variety of formations during descent. Formations with the canopies include two or more flying side by side, several stacked one on top of another, or one parachutist flying upside down with others nearby.

cave complex in the Shahi Khot Valley near Gardez, Afghanistan, as part of Operation Anaconda.

Al Qaeda terrorists fleeing from the 10th Mountain Division were blocked by the 101st Airborne Division at the north end of the valley. The hundreds of Taliban fighters were determined to hold their territory and tragically took eight American lives. In desperation, the Al Qaeda elements opened fire with rocket-propelled grenades, mortars, and machine-gun fire. In response, forward air controllers from the 101st Division directed massive air strikes from F-16 fighters and B-52 bombers; Apache helicopters provided close air support. One valiant Screaming Eagle soldier was killed during this raid, and several others were wounded. The Taliban forces dug in and continued to inhabit the area.

In the spring and summer of 2002 the 3rd Brigade, 101st Airborne Division, deployed to Afghanistan to provide security for Kandahar International Airport. The 101st units participated in the other major operations as well.

On February 6, 2003, units of the entire 101st Airborne Division, plus the 101st Corps Support Group and the 86th

Combat Actions of the 101st Airborne Division (Air Assault) in Operation Iraqi Freedom

Author's note: These are a sampling of the numerous patrols that the soldiers of the 101st Airborne Division (Air Assault) conducted during their most recent tour of duty in Operation Iraqi Freedom.

November 26, 2005—On a road south of Baghdad, soldiers from 2nd Brigade Combat Team, 101st Airborne Division, observed two Iraqi terrorists' IEDs in holes, collecting explosives from two houses in the surrounding area. As air support was called in to look closer at the situation, the men dove into a ditch to hide. Attack aviation helicopters engaged the terrorists, killing one and injuring the other. While clearing the area, soldiers from Company A, 2nd Battalion, 502nd Infantry Regiment, came across the IED, which had a detonation cord running up the road. An explosive ordnance disposal team called to the site detonated the device.

November 27, 2005—Military observers witnessed a group of terrorists with rocket propelled grenades in a vehicle at an abandoned school south of Baghdad. While en route to the abandoned schoolhouse to address the situation, the soldiers from Company A, 2nd Battalion, 502nd Infantry Regiment, were engaged by the enemy in two separate incidents. The patrol hit a roadside bomb. Later, the soldiers were engaged with small-arms fire from terrorists in a truck. The 101st Airborne Division soldiers returned fire, forcing the terrorists to flee the area. When the Company A soldiers reached the school, they spotted the two terrorists with command wires in their hands. On further inspection, the soldiers determined the wires were connected to a roadside bomb and detained the two terrorists for further questioning. An explosive ordnance disposal team was called to the site to assess and detonate the device.

November 30, 2005—Iraqi and U.S. troops from the 101st Airborne Division's 1st Brigade Combat Team spent weeks unearthing weapons from a major cache initially discovered November 27, 2005. The soldiers conducted a systematic excavation outside an abandoned military base near Kirkuk. They secured a large cache and several smaller caches nearby. Several thousand mortar rounds are removed from the site.

December 23, 2005—An air assault mission was conducted by 1st Battalion, 187th Infantry Regiment, 101st Airborne Division (Air Assault). The mission resulted in the capture of six terrorism suspects and the seizure of a large ammunition cache. Elements from Company C, 1st Battalion, 187th Infantry Regiment, landed in Muslakhah, north of Fatah, aboard UH-60 Blackhawk helicopters and began searching the village for individuals listed as being involved with terrorist activities in the area. During the air assault mission, soldiers of Company D, 1st Battalion, 187th Infantry Regiment, launched an amphibious assault on an island in the Tigris River adjacent to Muslakhah. While patrolling the banks of the island, they discovered a cache of forty-five 82-mm rounds and sixty-four 120-mm rounds. They also seized twenty rockets and six hundred rounds of small-arms ammunition.

December 27, 2005—U.S. Army UH-60 Blackhawk helicopter carries soldiers of the 101st Airborne Division to conduct an aerial assessment of an oil pipeline fire outside Forward Operating Base McHenry, Iraq.

January 26, 2006—Troops from the 3rd Brigade Combat Team, 101st Airborne Division, investigated the information provided by an Iraqi local and discovered two large artillery rounds placed in the hill.

February 22, 2006—Soldiers from the 2nd Battalion, 502nd Infantry Regiment, 2nd Brigade, 101st Airborne Division, found and destroyed another weapons cache southwest of Baghdad. This cache had mortar and artillery rounds, rockets, and mortar base plates.

February 23, 2006—Iraqi and coalition soldiers cleared a previously unidentified minefield near Tikrit, the result of a tip from a local man. The soldiers, from the 1st Brigade, 4th Iraqi Army Division, and the 3rd Brigade Combat Team, 101st Airborne Division, were searching the area for weapons caches when they came across the man, who guided them to the minefield. The joint U.S.-Iraqi team discovered and destroyed antipersonnel mines. Machine-gun ammunition and rifles also were confiscated.

March 23, 2006—In the Baghdad area, an Iraqi citizen led soldiers from the 2nd Battalion, 502nd Infantry Regiment, 2nd Brigade Combat Team, 101st Airborne Division, to a weapons cache, consisting of sixteen rocket propelled grenade rounds. Following its discovery, 101st Airborne Division soldiers began searching the area and found a second cache, consisting of twenty-four rocket propelled grenade rounds.

April 27, 2006—Near Tikrit, Iraq, a civilian kidnapped in Samarra was rescued when soldiers from 3rd Brigade Combat Team, 101st Airborne Division, stopped and searched three vehicles. In one of the silver sedans, American soldiers detained three occupants. In the trunk, soldiers discovered a bound-and-gagged kidnap victim, who was then transported to a medical facility for care.

May 10 and 11, 2006—During a nighttime aerial reconnaissance mission, helicopters from the 101st Combat Aviation Brigade, 101st Airborne Division, discovered two insurgents digging near a road in an effort to place a bomb. The aircrews shot both insurgents. A ground team of soldiers from 1st Battalion, 2nd Brigade, 4th Iraqi Army Division, and 1st Brigade Combat Team, 101st Airborne Division, moved into the area and confirmed that one insurgent was dead. The second was wounded but was not found at the site. The ground team discovered AK-47 assault rifles, hand grenades, and several ammunition magazines. The bomb was made up of artillery rounds and was destroyed in a controlled blast.

August 22, 2006—Soldiers from 4th Battalion, 320th Field Artillery Regiment, and 801st Brigade Support Battalion, 4th Brigade Combat Team, 101st Airborne Division, provided rice, beans, cooking oil, canned fish, blankets, vegetables, assorted condiments, cooking utensils, and stoves for displaced Iraqis in Zafaraniya outside the city Baghdad.

Soldiers of the C Company, 3rd Battalion, 187th Infantry Regiment, 101st Division, exit a CH-47 Chinook helicopter in Brassfield-Mora, Iraq, in support of Operation Swarmer, on March 16, 2006. *U.S. Navy photo by Photographer's Mate Third Class Shawn Hussong*

Combat Support Hospital, once again deployed in support of the war on terrorism. Within the week, the USNS *Dahl* and the USNS *Bob Hope* were loading military cargo in Jacksonville, Florida, the port for the 101st Airborne Division's movement. The ships' six-hundred-thousand-square-foot cargo capacities held Blackhawk, Apache, Kiowa, and Chinook helicopters and a variety of wheeled vehicles. While the

Sergeant Gustavo Gutierrez (front) and Specialist Roger Spain (back) from the Tigerforce Scout Platoon, 1-327th Infantry Regiment, 1st Brigade Combat Team, 101st Airborne Division (Air Assault), team up to pull security in the city of Hawijah, Iraq, during Operation Gaugamela, on July 20–21, 2006. *Photographer: Specialist Linsay Burnett, 1st Brigade Combat Team, 101st Airborne Division [AA] Public Affairs*

Above: Soldiers from Bravo Battery, 3rd Battalion, 320th Field Artillery Regiment, 101st Airborne Division, and soldiers from 4th Iraqi Army Division land in a field of black water during an operation close to a village in the western desert of Tikrit, Iraq, on April 30, 2006. *U.S. Army photo by Specialist Teddy Wade*

ships debarked for their sea voyage to the Persian Gulf, the first elements of the 101st Airborne Division boarded civilian aircraft on February 27, 2003, to deploy to Kuwait. The 101st Division continues to serve deployments to the Persian Gulf.

The 101st Airborne Division (Air Assault) officially initiated its organizational transformation efforts on September 16, 2004. As of June 2006, the division had reorganized into four brigade combat teams (units of action), two aviation brigade combat teams (the 101st Aviation Brigade and the 159th Aviation Brigade), and support units such as division artillery, division support command, corps support group, and several separate commands. The 101st Aviation Brigade and the 159th Aviation Brigade were transformed as well. The

101st Brigade was strictly an attack-helicopter brigade, while the 159th Brigade was an assault-helicopter brigade. Now, both aviation brigades comprise an attack battalion, an assault battalion, a cavalry squadron, a general-support aviation battalion, and an aviation-support battalion. Reorganizations and redeployments are in the Screaming Eagles' future.

Over the decades, the valiant soldiers of the 101st Airborne Division have faced adversity and enemies, thus forming a noble lineage. Today the division continues its service in the war against terrorism with direct actions in the Iraq deserts and mountains of Afghanistan. Although it now has an undeniable place in the world's history, the 101st Airborne Division continues to proudly meet its rendezvous with destiny.

Opposite: Soldiers from the 101st Airborne Division and Iraqi Army search for a weapons cache on a farm outside of Hawijah, Iraq, on January 4, 2006. The U.S. soldiers are attached to Alpha Company, 1st Battalion, 327th Infantry Regiment. *DOD photo by Specialist Timothy Kingston, U.S. Army*

Specialist Randall Jernigan from A battery, 4-320th Field Artillery Battalion, 101st Division, exits an abandoned building after searching for possible weapons caches during Operation Ten Bears in Zafaraniyah, Baghdad, on January 23, 2006. *U.S. Army photo by Specialist Teddy Wade*

Soldiers from the 33rd Cavalry Regiment, 3rd Brigade Combat Team, 101st Airborne Division, rescue a dog from a canal while conducting a reconnaissance mission near FOB Heider, Iraq, on August 16, 2006. *DOD photo by Staff Sergeant Russell Lee Klika, U.S. Army*

On April 7, 2003, General Tommy Franks, CENTCOM commander in chief, delivered encouraging words to the soldiers of 1st Brigade (Bastogne), 101st Airborne Division (Air Assault), in Najaf, Iraq, after handing out Bronze Stars to two noncommissioned officers. *Photo by Private First Class Joshua Hutcheson, division journalist*

Soldiers of the 1st Brigade Combat Team, 101st Airborne Division (Air Assault), and the 2nd Iraqi Army Division count the munitions unearthed in a network of caches discovered west of Kirkuk, Iraq.

Sergeant Antonio Montes and fellow military police officers from the 506th Regimental Combat Team, 101st Airborne Division, conduct a dismounted patrol through the neighborhood of Adhamiya in East Baghdad, Iraq, on June 26, 2006. *U.S. Navy photo by PH1 Bart A. Bauer*

Specialist Lilly Moreno and fellow soldiers from the "War Hawks" 506th Regimental Combat Team, 101st Airborne Division, provide perimeter security at the site of an improvised explosive device detonation in east Baghdad on May 10, 2006. Sailors from the U.S. Navy's explosive ordnance disposal unit (Mobile Unit 6, Detachment 10) conduct a postblast analysis of the site. *U.S. Navy photo by PH1 Bart A. Bauer*

Above: Corporal Brandon Helton operates an M240B machine gun and provides security for his platoon during Operation Iron Triangle in a desert area near Balad, Iraq, on May 9, 2006. Helton is assigned to C Company, 3-187th Infantry Regiment, 101st Airborne Division. *U.S. Army photo by Specialist Teddy Wade*

Left: An Iraqi border-patrol soldier takes a break after an early morning firefight with smugglers trying to cross into Iraq from Syria.

On January 11, 2006, soldiers from Bravo Company, 2nd Battalion, 502nd Infantry, continued Operation Falcon Sweep in the village of Shakaria, Iraq. One of the operation's objectives was to identify and detain terrorists in the village. Sergeant Isreal Rearica (right) gets guidance on where to place his soldiers when Blackhawk helicopters land. *U.S. Army photo by Staff Sergeant Kevin L. Moses Sr.*

Above: An AH-64D Longbow Apache, 1st Battalion, 101st Aviation Regiment, provides ground forces with air support from FOB Speicher, Iraq, on October 21, 2005. *U.S. Air Force photo by Technical Sergeant Andy Dunaway*

Left: Chief Warrant Officer Tom Scott, a UH-60A Blackhawk helicopter pilot deployed to the 1st Forward Support Medical Team, puts on his helmet before a mission near Tall Afar, Iraq, on August 1, 2006. Scott is assigned to the 542nd Medical Company (Air Ambulance). *U.S. Air Force photo by Staff Sergeant Jacob N. Bailey*

Flame erupts from a building hit with a TOW missile launched by soldiers of the 101st Airborne Division (Air Assault) on July 21, 2003, in Mosul, Iraq. Saddam Hussein's sons, Qusay and Uday, were killed in a gun battle as they resisted coalition forces' efforts to apprehend and detain them. *DOD photo by Specialist Robert Woodward, U.S. Army*

Soldiers of the 101st Airborne Division (Air Assault) crouch down and prepare themselves for the loud boom from the TOW missile that is going to be fired at a Mosul building in which Uday and Qusay Hussein have barricaded themselves on July 22, 2003. *U.S. Army photo by Sergeant Curtis Hargrave*

Left: Captain Adam Lackey, commander of Alpha Company, 1-187th Infantry Regiment, 3rd Brigade Combat Team, 101st Airborne Division (Air Assault), watches as four UH-60 Blackhawks arrive to extract soldiers after an early morning raid of Bayji Island, Iraq, on January 15, 2006. *U.S. Army photo by Specialist Jose Ferrufino*

Below: On January 11, 2006, soldiers from Bravo Company, 2nd Battalion, 502nd Infantry, continued Operation Falcon Sweep in the village of Shakaria, Iraq. Soldiers from the 101st maintain rooftop security as a fellow soldier sweeps the area. *U.S. Army photo by Staff Sergeant Kevin L. Moses Sr.*

Right: Staff Sergeant Calvin Newman maintains perimeter security for his fellow soldiers while on patrol in east Baghdad, Iraq, on March 15, 2006. Newman is attached to the 506th Regimental Combat Team, 101st Airborne Division. *U.S. Navy photo by PH1 Bart A. Bauer*

Below: Two AH-64D Longbow Apache helicopters return from a combat mission to FOB Speicher, Iraq, on October 22, 2005. The Apaches are attached to the 1st Battalion, 101st Aviation Regiment. *DOD photo by Technical Sergeant Andy Dunaway, U.S. Air Force*

Staff Sergeant Justin Orr, a squad leader for the Tigerforce Scout Platoon, 1-327th Infantry Regiment, 1st Brigade Combat Team, 101st Airborne Division (Air Assault), watches the city of Hawijah, Iraq, while pulling rooftop security during Operation Gaugamela, on July 20–21, 2006. An OH-58 Kiowa circles overhead.
Photographer: Specialist Linsay Burnett, 1st Brigade Combat Team, 101st Airborne Division [AA] Public Affairs

Soldiers with the 1st Battalion, 187th Infantry Regiment, 101st Airborne Division (Air Assault), in Serkankheil, Afghanistan, scan the nearby ridgeline for enemy movement during Operation Anaconda. *U.S. Army photo by Specialist David Marck Jr., 314th Press Camp Headquarters*

A U.S. Air Force B-52 aircraft takes off from a classified location on its way to Afghanistan in support of Operation Enduring Freedom, April 12, 2006. *U.S. Air Force photo by Senior Master Sergeant John Rohrer*

Warrior, a derivative of the combat-proven Predator, fully meets the U.S. Army's requirement for a low-risk developmental solution for persistent ISR and tactical strike operations. The aircraft provides long-endurance surveillance, communications relay, and weapons delivery missions, with double the weapons capacity of Predator. Featuring a heavy fuel engine (HFE) for increased supportability in the field, Warrior can fly above 25,000 feet on jet or diesel fuel with increased horsepower and fuel efficiency.

On August 31, 2003, soldiers of Headquarters, Headquarters Company, 3-502nd Infantry Regiment, 101st Airborne Division (Air Assault), mark the spot in a field where unexploded ordnance were found in Mosul, Iraq. *U.S. Army photo by Pvt. Daniel D Meacham*

Corporal Ramirez from Headquarters Platoon, Charlie Company, 1st Battalion, 187th Infantry Regiment, 101st Airborne Division, provides security during a raid in Siniya, Iraq, on April 12, 2006. *U.S. Army photo by Specialist Charles W. Gill*

Sergeant Christina Watkins, 402nd Civil Affairs Detachment, attached to the 101st Airborne Division, conducts a climate assessment of a marketplace in Tikrit, Iraq, on July 5, 2006. Climate assessments collect information about the needs and concerns of the citizens in the area. *U.S. Army photo by Staff Sergeant Russell Lee Klika*

Left: Private First Class William Mckenzie of the 1st Squadron, 33rd Cavalry Regiment, 3rd Brigade Combat Team, 101st Airborne Division, participates in Operation Starlit, a nine-day mission in the Salah Ad Din providence of Iraq. The mission was conducted to rid the area of anti-Iraqi forces.

Below: On December 30, 2005, soldiers from Bravo Company, 2nd Battalion, 502nd Infantry, conducted search and sweep operations in the village of Shakaria, Iraq. Soldiers from Bravo Company secured a road as an explosive ordnance disposal unit worked to disarm an IED that was buried on it. *U.S. Army photo by Staff Sergeant Kevin L. Moses Sr.*

Sergeant Jason Manley and fellow military police officers from the 506th Regimental Combat Team, 101st Airborne Division, conduct a dismounted patrol through the east Baghdad neighborhood of Adhamiya, on June 26, 2006. *U.S. Navy photo by PH1 Bart A. Bauer*

On February 9, 2006, Sergeant Mackenzie Verdi of the "War Hawks" Military Police unit, 506th Regimental Combat Team, 101st Airborne, and fellow detail members post security during visits to local reconstruction projects in east Baghdad. *U.S. Navy photo by PH1 Bart A. Bauer*

Staff Sergeant Justin Orr, a squad leader for the Tigerforce Scout Platoon, 1-327th Infantry Regiment, 1st Brigade Combat Team, 101st Airborne Division (Air Assault), watches the city of Hawijah, Iraq, while pulling rooftop security during Operation Gaugamela, on July 20–21, 2006. An OH-58 Kiowa circles overhead. *Photographer: Specialist Linsay Burnett, 1st Brigade Combat Team, 101st Airborne Division [AA] Public Affairs*

Sergeant Michael Goodson from A Battery, 4th Battalion, 320th Field Artillery Regiment, 101st Division, performs a foot patrol in search of possible weapons caches during Operation Ten Bears in the Zafaraniyah neighborhood of Baghdad on January 23, 2006. *U.S. Army photo by Specialist Teddy Wade*

Private First Class Janelle Zalkovsky of the Civil Affairs Unit, 1st Battalion, 320th Field Artillery Regiment, 101st Airborne, provides security while other soldiers survey a newly constructed road in Ibriam Jaffes, Iraq, on December 4, 2005. The road project was initiated by the Civil Affairs Unit in cooperation with local officials to provide better access to the village from other main travel routes. *U.S. Army photo by Specialist Charles W. Gill*

Soldiers conduct a patrol in Salah Ad Din, Iraq, on July 6, 2006, as part of a nine-day operation in search of insurgents. The soldiers are from 1st Squadron, 33rd Cavalry Regiment, 3rd Brigade Combat Team, 101st Airborne Division. *U.S. Army photo by Staff Sergeant Russell Lee Klika*

Two CH-47 Chinook helicopters head north toward Iraq from Camp Udairi, Kuwait, carrying soldiers with 3rd Battalion, 101st Aviation Regiment, 101st Airborne Division. The soldiers set up a forward fuel resupply point that would allow the division to conduct further air assaults deep into Iraq. *U.S. Army photo by Private First Class James Matise*

CH-47 Chinook helicopter crewmembers of the 101st Airborne Division converse on the flight line at Camp Udairi, Kuwait, shortly before flying across the border into Iraq. Meanwhile, AH-64 Apache helicopters wait to take off. *U.S. Army photo by Private First Class James Matise*

Soldiers of 1st Squadron, 33rd Cavalry Regiment, 3rd Brigade Combat Team, 101st Airborne Division, provide security as their platoon leader gathers intelligence along the Syria/Iraq border near FOB Nimur. *U.S. Army photo by Staff Sergeant Russell Lee Klika*

Two soldiers with the 101st Airborne Division (Air Assault) pull security during a raid on a suspected terrorist training camp in southwestern Iraq on September 10, 2003. *U.S. Army photo by Specialist Kieran Moore*

Opposite: Sergeant Gustavo Gutierrez, a team leader with the Tigerforce Scout Platoon, 1-327th Infantry Regiment, 1st Brigade Combat Team, 101st Airborne Division (Air Assault), takes a knee while watching the street during a cordon and search in a village in the Hawijah district of Iraq, on July 17–18, 2006. *Photographer: Specialist Linsay Burnett, 1st Brigade Combat Team, 101st Airborne Division [AA] Public Affairs*

Specialist Roger Spain (front) and Staff Sergeant Justin Orr (back) from the Tigerforce Scout Platoon, 1-327th Infantry Regiment, 1st Brigade Combat Team, 101st Airborne Division (Air Assault), provide protection from the roof of a building for soldiers on the ground during Operation Gaugamela in the city of Hawijah, Iraq, on July 20–21, 2006. *Photographer: Specialist Linsay Burnett, 1st Brigade Combat Team, 101st Airborne Division [AA] Public Affairs*

Right: Specialist Ted Trenary and Private First Class Kevin Tirserio (right) prepare to launch the Raven unmanned aerial vehicle at FOB McHenry, Iraq, on November 30, 2005. The soldiers, attached to Headquarters, Headquarters Company, 1st Battalion, 327th Infantry Regiment, 101st Airborne, are using the Raven to scan Route Trans-Am for improvised explosive devices. *DOD photo by Technical Sergeant Andy Dunaway, U.S. Air Force*

A soldier with Alpha Company, 1st Battalion, 187th Infantry Regiment, 3rd Brigade Combat Team, 101st Airborne Division, patrols in the market center in Bayji, Iraq.

Members of B Company, 1-502nd Infantry Battalion, 101st Airborne Division, move through an orchard during Operation Desert Scorpion. The operation was an effort to disrupt terrorist activities near Rushdie Mula, Iraq. The photo was taken on the morning of April 19, 2006. *U.S. Army photo by Sergeant 1st Class David D. Isakson*

Sergeant Leno Lemus from C Company, 3-187th Infantry Regiment, 101st Airborne Division, performs a ballistic bridge to open the door of a house, while the rest of his squad waits in a small village near the city of Balad, during the air-assault operation Iron Triangle on May 10, 2006. Operation Iron Triangle was conducted to find and kill most-wanted terrorists. *U.S. Army photo by Specialist Teddy Wade*

Corporal Jared Jenkins and First Sergeant Arthur Abiera, Apache Troop, 1st Squadron, 33rd Cavalry Regiment, 3rd Brigade Combat Team, 101st Airborne Division, search a home during a routine presence patrol on the outskirts of Sadr City, Iraq.

First Lieutenant Graham Genrich from B Battery, 3-320th Field Artillery, 101st Airborne Division, secures the perimeter with an M-4 rifle during a patrol in Osha City, Tikrit, on April 27, 2006. *U.S. Army photo by Specialist Teddy Wade*

Specialist Jason Palmer, a crew chief for a Blackhawk helicopter from A Company, 5th Battalion, 101st Aviation Regiment, prepares the crew and passengers for takeoff before an air-assault operation with units from FOB Remagen, Tikrit, on April 30, 2006. Operation Savage Strike was conducted by soldiers from 3-320th Field Artillery Regiment and Iraqi Army soldiers. *U.S. Army photo by Specialist Teddy Wade*

UH-60 Blackhawk helicopters arrive on FOB Dagger, Tikrit, on August 8, 2006. The helicopters are carrying VIPs attending a ceremony marking the 4th Iraqi Army Division taking the lead on security for the provinces of Sulymaniya, Salah Ah Din, and Kirkuk. *U.S. Army photo by Staff Sergeant Russell Lee Klika*

Specialist Shan Neiger and soldiers from the 101st Airborne Division take cover while a Chinook CH-47D helicopter from the 101st Combat Aviation Brigade lands in a desert location during the last hours of Operation Iron Triangle on May 11, 2006. *U.S. Army photo by Specialist Teddy Wade*

U.S. soldiers take cover during a gun battle with anticoalition forces on July 6, 2006, during a nine-day operation in the Salah Ad Din providence of Iraq. The soldiers are from 1st Squadron, 33rd Cavalry Regiment, 3rd Brigade Combat Team, 101st Airborne Division. *U.S. Army photo by Staff Sergeant Russell Lee Klika*

Command Sergeant Major Gregory Patton, from 1st Squadron, 33rd Cavalry Regiment, 3rd Brigade Combat Team, 101st Airborne Division, walks through a bombed-out building on July 6, 2006, after a firefight with insurgents in Salah Ad Din, Iraq. *U.S. Army photo by Staff Sergeant Russell Lee Klika*

Two soldiers from the 101st Airborne scan the area ahead of them prior to linking up with soldiers from the Iraqi Army in the village of Shumait, Iraq, on November 27, 2005. The U.S. soldiers from 1st Platoon, Alpha Company, 1st Battalion, 327th Infantry Regiment, 101st Airborne Division, conducted a joint foot patrol with Iraqi soldiers to show a presence and to search for insurgent activity. *DOD photo by Technical Sergeant Andy Dunaway, U.S. Air Force*

First Lieutenant Thomas Beyerl gives instructions to soldiers in his unit in the Adhamiyah area of northeast Baghdad on October 2, 2006. The soldiers were assigned to Alpha Troop, 1st Squadron, 61st Cavalry Regiment, 506th Regimental Combat Team, 101st Airborne Division. *DOD photo by Petty Officer Second Class Erik A. Wehnes, U.S. Navy*

UH-60 Blackhawk helicopters lift off from FOB Remagen, Iraq, for Operation Swarmer on March 16, 2006. Soldiers from the Iraqi Army's 1st Brigade, 4th Division, and the U.S. Army's 101st Airborne Division's 3rd Brigade Combat Team took part in the combined air-assault operation to clear the area northeast of Samarra of suspected insurgents. *DOD photo by Sergeant First Class Antony Joseph, U.S. Army*

Right: A plume of smoke surrounds a UH-60 Blackhawk helicopter, as soldiers of the 101st Airborne Division conduct an aerial assessment of an oil pipeline fire outside FOB McHenry, Iraq, on Decemeber 27, 2005. *DOD photo by Specialist Timothy Kingston, U.S. Army*

Acknowledgments

No project of magnitude is completed alone, and *Screaming Eagles* was no different. With immense gratitude, I thank my editor Steve Gansen for his persistent support and encouragement. His attention to detail has given this publication its added edge. I appreciate my wife, Susan, for writing another text while maintaining a career and raising children. I'd also like to thank my children Morgan and Travis for their continued interest and patience, and our yellow lab Tybee for her constant companionship at the computer. Most importantly, I gratefully thank the patriotic men and women of the 101st Airborne Division who freely give of themselves as defenders of our great nation.

—Russ Bryant

Index

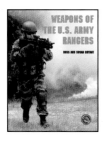

**Weapons of the U.S. Army
Rangers**
ISBN-10 0-7603-2112-4
ISBN-13 978-0-7603-2112-6

U.S. Air Force Special Ops
ISBN-10 0-7603-2947-8
ISBN-13 978-0-7603-2947-4

Red Flag
ISBN-10 0-7603-2530-8
ISBN-13 978-0-7603-2530-8

To Be a Paratrooper
ISBN-10 0-7603-3046-8
ISBN-13 978-0-7603-3046-3

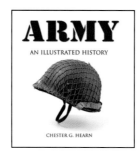

Army
ISBN-10 0-7603-2680-0
ISBN-13 978-0-7603-2680-0

Wounded Soldier, Healing Warrior
ISBN-10 0-7603-3113-8
ISBN-13 978-0-7603-3113-2

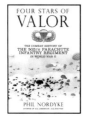

Four Stars of Valor
ISBN-10 0-7603-2664-9
ISBN-13 978-0-7603–2664-0

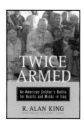

Twice Armed
ISBN-10 0-7603-2386-0
ISBN-13 978-0-7603-2386-1

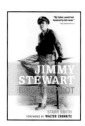

Jimmy Stewart: Bomber Pilot
ISBN-10 0-7603-2824-2
ISBN-13 978-0-7603-2824-8